362 7 THOB

P/O NO:
ACCESSION NO: KHO1120
SHELFMARK: 362.73/THO

KU-559-352

Success and Failure in Permanent Family Placement

JUNE THOBURN
School of Economic and Social Studies
University of East Anglia

Avebury

Aldershot · Brookfield USA · Hong Kong · Singapore · Sydney

© J. Thoburn, 1990

All rights reserved. No part of this publication may be reproduced,   ıced,
stored in a retrieval system, or transmitted in any form or by any   any
means , electronic, mechanical, photocopying, recording or otherwise   rwise
without the prior permission of Gower Publishing Company Limited

Published by
Avebury
Gower Publishing Company Limited
Gower House
Croft Road
Aldershot
Hants GU11 3HR
England

Gower Publishing Company
Old Post Road
Brookfield
Vermont 05036
USA

Reprinted 1997

British Library Cataloguing in Publication Data
Thoburn, June, 1939-
    Success and failure in permanent family placement.
    1. Children.   Foster care
    I. Title
    362.7'33

ISBN   0 566 07080 4

Printed in Great Britain by Antony Rowe Ltd., Chippenham, Wiltshire

362.73/THO

HSE South Kerry General Hospital
Library

KH01120

Contents

Acknowledgements

I have been privileged, over the last seven years, to be involved in some of the exciting and hopeful changes which have been taking place in thinking about how best to meet the needs of deprived children. Many conversations with social work and research colleagues have taken my ideas forward, and I single out for special thanks Joan Fratter, Pauline Hoggan, Gerry O'Hara, Roy Parker, Jane Rowe and John Triseliotis. I should like to thank also Anne Murdoch and Alison O'Brien, my research colleagues for the earlier phase of this study. Both have been generous with their time when I needed to check out my perceptions, and Alison has helped with the assessment of some of the younger children at the five year stage.

All my colleagues at UEA have provided encouragement and constructive comment, but I owe a special debt of gratitude to Peter Wedge who, first as a member of the rsearch advisory group and then as supervisor of my MSW dissertation, was always there when needed with ideas, encouragement and the illusive turn of phrase. Anne Borrett brought her expertise and patience to bear on my manuscript, and I thank her for that and the many services she gives so willingly.

Thanks are due also to John, Nick and Alan for providing the warmth and good humour which have nurtured me when pressures were at risk of getting out of hand.

But most importantly, I acknowledge that this book could not have been written without the parents, young people, and Children's Society social workers who have shared their thoughts and feelings with me over the past six or seven years. I am grateful to them all for their time, patience and tolerance in allowing me to intrude and helping me to make

sense of the process which had such a profound impact on all their
lives. They did so in the hope that other children in need of new
families, and other families who were considering taking a special child
into their homes would benefit from their experiences. Any one of their
stories could have filled a book in its own right. I have attempted to
pick out those themes, and words of wisdom or warning, which others will
find most helpful. Many of the words which follow, and most of the
ideas, are theirs. The responsibility for selecting and drawing out the
themes is mine, and I alone take responsibility for any errors and
omissions.

1 Permanent family placement in context

In recent years most local authority social services departments have issued child care policy statements based on the need to provide "permanence" for the children in their care. Typically, they contain comments such as this from a Kent County Council leaflet sent to all foster parents in 1987:

> It is very difficult to meet these needs [for love and security] when children are in long-term local authority care, which is why the Department's policy is to place for permanence.

Although "permanence" has figured highly in child care literature and thinking from the mid 1970s, it was not until the early 1980s that substantial numbers of children in care were placed with permanent substitute families. Thus, it is only recently that large enough numbers of children have been in placement for long enough for an evaluation to be attempted of a policy which has already become a central plank in the provision of services for children in care. It is the purpose of this book to make such an attempt by drawing together the conclusions of evaluative studies on the subject, paying particular attention to the different definitions of success, and by considering in detail the progress of 21 children during the first five years of their lives with their new families.

Before evaluating any new policy it is important to consider why the change is thought to be necessary, and what benefits are expected to accrue from it.

Child care policy in Britain since 1948, as several authors, most notably Packman (1981), have pointed out, has moved through several phases. The decade to the late fifties was characterised by an enthusiasm about the possibilities of state agencies rescuing children from a range of inappropriate living situations - from neglectful families, from Poor Law institutions, from ill-supervised and exploitative foster homes, and from establishments with harsh disciplinary regimes. John Stroud's The Shorn Lamb (1960) conveys a sense of the mission of the child care officers of that period to humanise the institutions of the state in order to provide a high standard of care for children in need who were unable to live with their own families. By the late fifties this enthusiasm was somewhat blunted by reality, and it was increasingly acknowledged that there were many obstacles in the way of local authorities providing for the long-term needs of children in their care.

In the sixties, hopes were pinned on "prevention", with Section 1 of the 1963 Children and Young Persons Act giving official blessing to those who were already working towards a service which enhanced the ability of natural families to give good enough care to their children. In the terminology of today, permanence was to be achieved for most children by keeping them with their own families. The rhetoric of prevention, however, was never backed up with adequate resources. The voluntary agencies such as Family Service Units continued their work, and some local authorities provided resources for preventive social work at the "tertiary" prevention level (see Parker, 1980, for a discussion of primary, secondary and tertiary prevention). However, preventive services were patchy and had hardly got off the ground before social work became embroiled in the re-organisation recommended by the Seebohm Committee (HMSO, 1968).

Meanwhile, in America, social services agencies and politicians had come to the conclusion reached in Britain ten years earlier that state services had their limitations when it came to caring for children, and in particular that they were rarely able to meet the needs of children for security, stability, and loving care which should be available to them throughout their childhood. The American response was to develop "permanence policies", and several demonstration projects were set up to test out the proposition that well-resourced social work agencies could move children from public care to placements with families (which might be the birth families or substitute families) which in Maluccio and Fein's (1983, p.197) terms offered "continuity of relationships with nurturing parents or caretakers and the opportunity to establish life-time relationships". The most novel aspect of these policies was the placement for adoption of children who had previously been considered unadoptable, principally older children and those with physical or mental disabilities, or emotional and behaviour difficulties.

In Britain a series of tragedies, such as the death of Maria Colwell at the hands of her step-father, alongside disquiet at the high rate of foster home breakdowns, and the realisation that many children were drifting for years in unplanned care (Rowe and Lambert, 1973), led to another rethink of policy and to the 1975 Children Act. Workers looked across the Atlantic and it was the adoption aspects of permanence policies which captured their imagination.

The combination of enthusiastic social workers and adoption agencies, and the shortage of healthy, white babies for adoption, had already ensured that some children previously thought unadoptable were being placed with adoptive families, (especially those from minority ethnic groups or children of mixed parentage, and children under five whose parents were requesting adoption but where the youngster had a disability, or where there was a risk of disability, or mental health problems). (See particularly Raynor, 1970, and Tizard, 1977.) The Association of British Adoption Agencies, (now The British Agencies for Adoption and Fostering - BAAF) had encouraged this extension to the ranks of adoptable children, and played a major part in making available in Britain knowledge about the work of the pioneering American adoption agencies. Kay Donley toured Britain in 1974 giving a series of lectures about the work of Spaulding for Children (Donley, 1975), and several British adoption workers visited America.

There are several reasons why it was the adoption side of American permanence policies which captured the imagination of British workers rather more than the rehabilitation side. Inevitably there is more enthusiasm for new ideas than for those which have been tried and deemed not to work. Prevention and rehabilitation in Britain seemed to have a rather faded look about them by this stage, whereas placement for adoption of special needs children presented new challenges, and offered new ways of working. Whatever the reason, when the opening of the Barnardo's New Families Project in Glasgow in 1976 heralded in a decade in which permanence policies would dominate progressive thinking about meeting the needs of children in care, it was the adoption aspects of permanence which were to the fore, at the expense of the preventive and rehabilitative aspects. Such policies, it was hoped, would minimise "drift" in unplanned care and cut down the numbers of young people leaving care at 18 who were attached to neither their birth families nor to substitute families.

Until fairly recently, permanence policies have relied for their justification on reported successes in individual cases, and on the enthusiasm of the pioneers, mostly in adoption agencies and children's societies in the voluntary sector, or in adoption sections of local authorities such as Lothian (see McKay, 1980; O'Hara and Hoggan, 1988) and Lambeth (see Hussel and Monaghan, 1982). As part of its work in evaluating its own projects, Barnardo's published reports on its Glasgow project in 1977 (Lindsay-Smith and Price, 1977, and Kerrane et al., 1981). Other workers, especially those employed by Parents for Children, a London-based agency specialising in the placement of children with severe handicaps, produced valuable accounts of their work and became heavily involved in training, thus making it possible for new specialist placement units to be set up (Sawbridge, 1980). The Annual Reports of these agencies also provided useful material about the number of placements being made, and about the children and new families. The numbers of children placed annually grew and during 1987 details were collected on 1,165 children who had been placed by 24 voluntary agencies between 1980 and 1985. Quantitative material from this survey (Thoburn and Rowe, 1988) will be introduced in order to provide background information against which to set the 21 children studied in detail.

Before moving on to an evaluation of permanent family placement, it is necessary first to consider precisely what is meant by the terms "special needs" and "permanent family placement".

The terms "special needs" and "hard-to-place" are used almost inter-changeably in the literature to cover groups of children with very different needs and backgrounds. The first group comprises those whose parents request adoption, but who would not in the past have been considered adoptable, either because they were beyond infancy, or because they had particular handicaps or special needs which meant that it would not be easy to find an adoptive home for them. Such children in previous years would have been received into care, and possibily placed with a view to adoption sometimes after fairly lengthy stays in care until the prognosis for their physical or mental development could be more accurately assessed. While most such children are placed from care, some are placed directly for adoption.

The second major group of children with special needs can be characterised as the "children who wait" described by Rowe and Lambert (1973). These will typically be children received into care several years earlier. They may have returned home to their parents on one or more occasions, and are likely also to have had several placements in care, including residential and foster homes, some of which may have been intended to be permanent. Some may also have been placed previously in adoptive homes which have disrupted. Many of these children will no longer be in touch with their parents, and others will have tenuous and ambivalent attachments to them. They are often older, and often include groups of siblings. As permanence policies begin to have an effect, such children will decrease in numbers, and this indeed seems to have happened. (See Wedge's (1986) account of the establishment of "permanence" units in Essex).

A third group of children with special needs will be those in care for shorter periods. Attempts are likely to have been made to rehabilitate these youngsters. Many will have been abused or neglected, but still have attachments, however ambivalent, to their birth families.

Special mention must also be made of the placement needs of children from minority ethnic groups who may come into any of these three categories. These children have special needs arising from the importance of maintaining their sense of racial, cultural and religious identity, and also need families who will help them to cope with the institutional racism which they are likely to meet in our society. Having been seen as unadoptable in the early days of the child care service, they were removed from this category when it was shown to be possible to place black babies and toddlers with (mostly) white families (Raynor, 1970). However, in recent years a re-assessment of trans-racial adoptive placements is leading policy-makers to the conclusion that placements should be sought with families of the same cultural, religious and racial background. There is some dispute amongst adoption workers about how easy it is to find such families, and therefore as to whether babies and toddlers from minority ethnic groups or of mixed parentage should again be considered as having special needs.

Table 1 gives an indication of the special needs of the children placed by the voluntary agencies surveyed by Thoburn and Rowe. Examples of "other problems" would be babies born as a result of incest, babies who have AIDS, or those sad cases where the children would need to come to terms with the fact that one parent was murdered by the other.

Table 1
Handicaps or special needs

	Number of children	Percentage
Down's Syndrome	92	8
Other mental handicap	107	9
Disabling physical handicap	92	8
Serious ill-health	62	5
Child experienced multiple moves	695	60
Child institutionalised	343	29
A history of deprivation or abuse	675	58
At least one disrupted "permanent" placement	254	22
Behaviour difficulties	591	51
Emotional difficulties	737	63
Other problems	261	23
Special needs, e.g. religious/cultural	136	12
Need to remain in contact with natural parent(s)	230	20
Need to remain in contact with siblings placed elsewhere or relatives	298	26
Need for family to cope with contested adoption	360	31
Member of a sibling group to be placed together	463	40
Older child (aged 9+ at placement)	465	40

Thoburn and Rowe (1988)

PERMANENT SUBSTITUTE FAMILIES

Permanence policies have become part of child care practice, not because "permanence" is a "good" in itself, but because of what it offers to the children in care - principally security, stability, and the opportunity to stay in one place for long enough to love and be loved and to make lasting relationships. The benefits of permanence are best summed up by Triseliotis's phrase "a family for life, with its network of support systems not only for them but also their future children" (Triseliotis, 1983, p.24). Whilst a proportion of children in care (and perhaps a larger proportion than we are currently willing to admit) did indeed find such families when placed in foster care before the introduction of permanence policies, this was often an unintended but fortunately happy outcome of policies which set out to keep children in care for as short a length of time as possible.

Vernon and Fruin (1986) and Millham et al. (1986) graphically describe how easily short-term placements drift on unless determined parents or social workers do something about getting the children home. Rowe and her colleagues (1984) pick up the story by describing a group of children at least five years after they joined their long-term foster families. Although the majority of these placements were viewed as de facto adoption placements, they have to be seen against a background of legislation and administrative rules which were formulated on the assumption that children's stay in care would be temporary. Thus, for example, the boarding-out regulations and the review process which requires that the possibility of return home should be considered every six months for children in statutory care, and the discouragement of children from using the name of their foster family and calling the foster parents "Mummy" and "Daddy", all combined to give a sense of impermanence. Triseliotis (1983, p.26) has described the effect of such policies as "constructed insecurity" and it can be hypothesised that this insecurity felt by many long-term foster parents and their children contributed to a breakdown rate estimated by Rowe (1983) as being somewhere between 20 and 40 per cent. Certainly this high breakdown rate, and the sense of insecurity of those in long-term foster care were strong reasons for advocating permanence policies. The major change when such policies were introduced was the placement of children in care with new families specifically with the intention that these would be permanent placements. In the early days, this usually meant placement with adoptive families, and the previous policy of placing children in foster families "with a view to adoption" became frowned upon. The Kent leaflet to foster parents, although perhaps more strongly worded than policies of other authorities, states a view currently held by many:

> For children coming into care after the issue of this policy statement, long-term fostering will almost never be the preferred plan. ... No child who comes into care under the age of 10 should remain in care for more than 2 years except in the most exceptional circumstances and with the written agreement of the Area Director. ... Neither wardship nor custodianship can offer the assurance of permanence and security within which substitute parents and child can make a commitment to each other.

However, many of the specialist placement agencies have learned from experience that all children are not adoptable, and increasingly are making placements with new families which may or may not lead to adoption. Thus the types of "permanent substitute family" to be evaluated in this monograph include foster and adoptive placements, and could in theory include custodianship, although such placements are still very few in number. Our main concern is not, however, with those families who started off as foster families, typically those described by Rowe and her colleagues (1984), where the intention was originally that the placement should be short-stay or of indeterminate duration, but where growing attachments led to a decision that it would become a permanent placement. This is an important distinction when evaluating

6

success since clearly there is likely to be a higher success rate amongst children and parents who have already grown to love each other and then decide to commit themselves permanently to each other, as compared with children and substitute parents who are artificially brought together with the intention that this should from the start be a permanent placement. An approximate analogy is the difference between living together for some time and deciding to get married, and the practice of arranging marriages between people who barely know each other which is the norm in some communities. Of the 1,165 children referred to in Table 1, three-quarters of those still in placement after between 18 months and six years had been adopted, around 8 per cent were still fostered with a view to adoption, and 15 per cent were permanently fostered.

A further reason for making a distinction between "mainstream" long-term foster placements which become permanent, and placements, whether in foster or adoptive homes, which, from the start, are intended to be permanent, is that the style of social work practice for the two is very different. Specifically, practice with foster families intended from the start to be permanent is hardly distinguishable from practice with adoptive families in that the aim from the start is to empower the new parents and create a "sense of permanence".

Another variable when considering the nature of placement with substitute families is whether the child loses total contact with members of the birth family, or remains in touch with birth parents, siblings, or other relatives. Just over a quarter of those children in our quantitative study whose placements had not disrupted were still in contact with members of their birth families.

Finally, there is the question of the point at which the child's status is considered. Recent studies show that some children are adopted many years after the placement, including a surprising number who are adopted at the ages of sixteen or seventeen.

Our survey of the 1,165 placements made by the voluntary agencies indicates that the rhetoric of permanence is indeed being put into practice. The partnership between the voluntary agencies and local authorities is still important, and the role of the voluntary societies in pioneering and publicising this work has been significant. However, the majority of local authorities are now undertaking their own permanent placement work so that numbers placed will now be very much greater. It is against this background of evidence of a substantial change in the practice of child placement that what must still be essentially an interim evaluation of the effectiveness of such policies should be set. Whilst surveys can tell us how many children are placed and give some details about their backgrounds, small-scale qualitative studies are needed in order to explore why some placements seem to be more successful than others, and to include more detailed information about the impact on the lives of the children, the new parents, and their own children. Nor can surveys tell us a great deal about the nature of the social work service offered, other than the type of placement made. Chapter 4 offers a detailed consideration of the lives of 21 children who were placed permanently five years previously and of their new families. Before narrowing the focus in this way, it is first necessary to consider the relevant literature and in particular to consider the question which until now has been begged - what do we mean by success?

7

2 Overview of evaluative research on adoption and long-term foster care

Reference will be made in Chapter 3 to the problems of methodology in evaluating success in family placement. However, it is important at this stage to consider the definitions of success which have been used in the different research studies. In order to arrive at a measure of success, it is important to start from the aims of those placing children for adoption or with permanent foster families. A glance through the literature, and the local authority policy statements serves to confirm that the major aim is that the youngster should stay in the placement until reaching independence and remain attached to the family well into adult life. Thus it seems appropriate to evaluate success primarily in terms of whether the placement lasted. As we shall see, few studies have been able to establish reliable breakdown rates, partly because prospective studies can rarely follow youngsters through for more than two or three years, because of expense. On the other hand, studies which pick up a group of adopted people, either several years after adoption or even in adult life, rarely include representative samples of those placements which did not last. A note is needed about terminology. Sometimes researchers and practitioners use "failure", "breakdown", "disruption", "dissolution" inter-changeably for any permanent removal from placement. At other times, "disruption" applies only to removal after placement and before legal adoption, and "dissolution" refers to removal after legal adoption.

It is not, however, enough to establish that the youngster remained in placement, if it is not clear that "permanence" in any particular case has indeed contributed to "well-being". Thus, most studies attempt to evaluate the youngsters' well-being at the point of interview, and some

- especially longitudinal studies - are able to make comparisons with the time of placement. Since many youngsters have been seriously damaged by their earlier life experience, it seems more appropriate to see success in comparative terms, either comparing the youngster with him or herself at the time of placement, or with a population of children who remained in care and were not placed with permanent new families. "Well-being" is sometimes assessed globally, the researcher listening to the evidence of the parents and/or the social worker and/or the children, and sometimes scrutinising social work records. Sometimes only the parents' view or the child or young person's view of "well-being" is used. Sometimes teachers are asked to rate the child both in terms of educational performance, and adjustment in school, and sometimes general practitioners are contacted for their views about the youngsters' health and development. In some studies the researcher has professional skills in assessing children, and interactions between the parents and children during the research interview are brought into the assessment. Self-esteem inventories and intelligence tests are also used in some studies. With such a variety of ways of assessing well-being, it is not easy to compare one study with another, although this process is aided in the British studies since most use the "Rutter" parent and/or teacher social adjustment scales as part of the assessment process (Rutter, 1975).

Research into children placed away from home has also indicated that a sense of personal identity is an important element of well-being, particularly as the youngster moves into adult life. This is being confirmed by studies of post-adoption centres, who report that a substantial proportion of those seeking help are adults who have problems which revolve around their sense of identity (Howe, 1987). Some studies have included assessment of this sense of identity, most notably those researching the placement of black children with white families, when racial identity becomes an issue.

The third main source of evidence about success comes from the consumers themselves. Most studies include the satisfaction with the adoption of the mother, sometimes the father, and sometimes the youngster, as part of the overall assessment of success; some use this as the only criterion on the basis that if the principal caretaker finds the experience satisfying, this is likely to be a major determinant of the child's well-being (Kadushin, 1970).

Finally, the success of agencies can be judged in terms of the proportion of children in need of permanent family placement who were actually placed, and whether those with the most severe "handicaps to placement" are being successfully established with permanent new families.

A REVIEW OF THE EVALUATION LITERATURE

Because permanent family placement as we have defined it is comparatively new, evaluative studies specifically of these new policies are limited, and most are American. There is a considerable body of practice literature, and in some of these studies practitioners offer modest but useful evaluations of their own practice, principally in terms of numbers and types of children placed. Whilst rich in descriptive material, such studies tell us little about the impact of the placements on the children, and rarely follow the youngsters for periods of years after placement. Other studies will therefore be included, which, whilst not specifically about permanent family placement as defined above, nonetheless consider populations of children similar to those with which we are concerned. These studies will be considered in terms of what they tell us about:

- the types of children placed and those referred but not placed

- the types of permanent placements studied

- the measures used to evaluate the placements and definitions of "success"

- the results reported in terms of success rates

- the reasons identified for placements either breaking down or being successful.

The studies are also rich in detail about the families and the ways in which they seek to integrate the newcomer, but the focus here will be on their evaluative aspects. They fall roughly into two groups.

Retrospective studies of young adults provide more useful evaluative information in that they are able to take a longer term view of success; on the other hand, they are based on models of practice which predate the style of work with which we are essentially concerned, and describe populations of children which are somewhat different. Most such studies evaluate placements of babies, and in most cases the natural parents were either requesting or at least not opposing placement for adoption.

The second group of studies consists of more recent accounts of children placed as a result of permanent placement policies. Thus they have the advantage of being more directly relevant to our study, but suffer the disadvantage that the length of time in placement on which to base an evaluation is frequently limited. The studies differ also in terms of whether they were undertaken "in house" with the practitioners describing or evaluating their own work, or whether they were undertaken by independent researchers; and also in terms of whether they are descriptive, evaluative, or both. Evaluative studies may be either longitudinal, following populations of children for varying lengths of time, or retrospective, looking back over the careers of youngsters who have been in placement for variable lengths of time. The size of the populations studied also varies considerably, from fewer than 20 children to over 1,500.

Thus whilst a glance through bibliographies would lead one to believe that much is known about populations of adopted children, the evidence about success is fragmented, and sometimes contradictory. This applies even to the placement for adoption of babies and toddlers, and is even more the case when we come to consider the permanent placement of children with special needs. Thus, Maza (1985), a statistician of the Administration for Children, Youth and Families, in the USA, after reviewing adoption statistics, comments:

National statistics that are being cited in the media on these and other aspects of adoption are based, at best, on small-scale research studies and scattered reports from States that do not use common definitions and, at worst, on 'guesses' derived from anecdotal information from workers in the field. Thus, these statistics must be handled carefully when they are used to inform adoption policy and practice decisions.

Given that permanence policies have been in operation in Britain for even shorter periods of time, this warning must be even more applicable to the British scene. In the following sections an attempt will be made to summarise the studies which are available. Appendix 1 lists the major studies on the placement of "special needs" children in terms of the success rates and the definitions of success used.

Before turning to studies of permanent family placement of children with special needs, we consider the studies of general populations of adopted children and also of children in long-term care who have special needs which provide important background information.

EVALUATIVE STUDIES OF ADOPTION

The majority of adoption studies describe the characteristics of adoptive families and adoptees and seek to tease out in what respects adoptive parenthood is different from parenting a natural child, and whether adoptive children differ from "natural" children. Perhaps the best known of these is Kirk's (1964) study in which he expounds his "shared fate" theory of the adoption experience. According to Kirk, successful adoption is likely to be related to whether parents and children openly acknowledge the adoption experience as being different from the birth experience, thus facilitating parental empathy with the child and freeing parents to allow youngsters to enquire about their origins, and making for easier communication between them. Such studies provide valuable information, but cannot provide information about success rates in the sense that by definition they omit those placements from which the youngsters were removed.

Pringle (1966), Jacka (1973), Clarke and Clarke (1976), Clarke (1981), Hapgood (1984) and Shaw (1984 and 1988) summarise studies which seek to evaluate success in adoptive placements, either in terms of breakdown rates or well-being.

Evaluative studies from outside Britain are those of Bohman (1970) and Bohman and Sigvardsson (1978 and 1980), who followed up a representative sample of 168 children placed as babies for adoption in Sweden. Control groups of children returned to birth parents and also in foster care, and a sample drawn from the general population of children were also used in this study, and success was based both on objective factors such as school performance, and on satisfaction levels of the parents. The children were studied at the ages of 11, 15, 18 and 23. At 11 it was found that whilst the girls were no more likely to be disturbed than the girls in the control group, more maladjustment was noted amongst the boys, whether adopted, fostered or returned home. There was an overall disturbance rate of 22 per cent compared with 12 per cent amongst a control group of classmates. At the age of 15 differences were described as of little consequence for the adopted group, but those fostered or returned home were still more likely than those in the control group to be maladjusted. About 80 per cent of the boys were followed up at 18 via the military enlistment procedure, which involved educational, health and psychological tests. The findings confirmed those for the boys when aged 15. However, at 23, when a search of

11

criminal offences of the sample was made, it was found that on this measure there was no difference between the controls, the adopted children and those raised by biological parents, but that those brought up in foster care were more likely to have had criminal offences, especially alcohol related offences, recorded against them. The authors hypothesise that a contributory factor may well have been that, although most remained from aged 9-months until adulthood in the same foster family, "there was legal and psychological insecurity connected with the placement, as there was no guarantee that the child could not some day be moved back again to the biological mother" (Bohman and Sigvardsson, 1980, p.31). A study by Jaffee and Fanshel (1970) reports on 100 adoptions between 20 and 30 years after placement. On the basis of interviews with the adoptive parents 33 per cent were rated as "low problem" and 34 per cent were classified as "middle range", with 33 per cent rated as "high problem" adoptees.

In Britain the major studies of young people adopted as infants are the retrospective ones of McWhinnie (1967), Kornitzer (1968) and Raynor (1980), and the prospective studies of Seglow et al. (1972) and Lambert and Streather (1980). Kornitzer and Raynor consider the satisfaction of both parents and children, Raynor finding that 80 per cent of the 160 adoptees expressed satisfaction with their upbringing, and 85 per cent of the adopters were satisfied or very satisfied with the adoption experience. Objective measures of well-being such as employment and satisfactory relationships with friends and partners are also used. Kornitzer studied 164 families including many de facto adoptions. Some were still children, but 62 adult adoptees were included. On the basis of her interviews she concluded that 75 per cent of these 62 placements were successful. McWhinnie's study involved lengthy interviews with 52 adopted adults and six adults who were permanently fostered. Her source of information was the adoptees and in some cases the family doctor. Objective measures were also used such as health, school and work records. Twenty-one of the 52 adoptees were assessed as having a good or fairly good adjustment, but this applied to only one of the six permanent foster children. Twenty-one were having severe problems in their upbringing which was related in some way to the adoption situation. This study differs from the others in that the success rate is somewhat lower, and that it covers placements made over a longer period of time, the interviewees varying in age between 18 and 60. The sample was mainly collected via GPs and this may have introduced bias which might explain the less positive results.

One of the more important recent British studies of children placed mainly for adoption as babies is that reported by Seglow et al. (1972) and Lambert and Streather (1980), which was a part of the National Child Development Study conducted by the National Children's Bureau. Since the 145 adopted children were part of a much larger cohort, a ready-made comparison group was available. At the age of seven they were in many respects making a better adjustment than the illegitimate children in the sample who had remained with their mothers and compared favourably with their peers in the general population. Using a range of tests, 70 per cent of the placements were described as satisfactory and 20 per cent as fairly satisfactory. This study notes that adopted children tend to be "advantaged" in material terms, especially when compared to their control group of children born illegitimately who remained with their birth parents. At 11 they were still doing better in most respects, either than the "illegitimately born" controls, or the legitimate children. However, when socially disadvantaging circumstances are controlled for, Lambert and Streather (p.133) report that "adopted children's social adjustment was poorer than that of legitimate children, and showed signs of having deteriorated relative to that of other children since the age of 7."

Of more relevance to this monograph are studies of children who, although placed some time ago, come into one of our "special needs" categories. These are principally of children placed when older or of children from minority ethnic groups, mostly placed trans-racially. The most important of these is Kadushin's (1970) study of 91 adoptive families of children placed between the ages of five and eleven. All the children were white and of average intelligence. They had no particular handicaps except that many had had several previous placements in care and experienced neglect or ill-treatment. The families were interviewed between six and ten years after placement. Using the satisfaction of the adopters as evidence of success, Kadushin rated 78 per cent of these placements as successful. Another American study which is of interest is a descriptive account by Powell (1984) of lengthy interviews with 17 adults, all of whom were over three at placement. Many retained contact with their birth families. This is a descriptive rather than an evaluative study, but the conclusions are nevertheless of interest. Powell concludes that:

> the data imply that older children are far more vulnerable to the stress of separation and placement than may be outwardly apparent. ... the importance of biological siblings and adoptive and birth extended families is revealed in the data. Involving children in the adoptive experience seems vital. ... when given choice, preparation, and participation, older children seem to be able to have a satisfying adoptive experience. When denied these opportunities, there tends to be dissatisfaction with adoption (pp.108-109).

It is of interest that 16 out of the 17 participants had contacted their birth families as young adults, but had principally retained contact with siblings rather than with parents.

Children placed for adoption when older have been studied in Britain by Triseliotis and Russell (1984) and by Tizard (1977) and Hodges and Tizard (1989). Triseliotis and Russell found that 82 per cent of 44 young adult adoptees, who were placed between the ages of two and ten, rated their growing up experience positively. (Interestingly, a similar rate to those placed as babies referred to above.) Using the adoptees' satisfaction with their growing-up experience and objective measures such as alcohol abuse, criminal records, adjustment in later life, the researchers rated over 80 per cent as successful.

Tizard considered five groups of children who spent the first two years of their lives in institutional care and were respectively returned home at two or around 5-years (22 children); placed for adoption at two or around 5-years (30 children); or placed in long-term foster care (5 children). Numbers for the latter group are very small, and it should also be noted that those returning home had originally been rejected by their birth mothers who had asked that they be adopted, and were mostly returned to adverse physical environments. The children were followed up at the ages of 8 (Tizard, 1977) and 16 (Hodges and Tizard, 1989). There was a comparison group of children who had never lived for any substantial period away from biological families. The researchers found that the adopted children succeeded better than the restored children in establishing close attachments with their parents or substitute parents. However, both at 8 and 16 the adopted children had more difficulty than the comparison group in getting on with peers and other adults outside the family, and these difficulties were reported by parents, teachers, and, at 16, the adolescents themselves.

Other researchers on the effectiveness of adoption have concentrated on the placement of black children, either within their own countries or between countries. Most such children have been placed trans-racially, and as babies, although increasingly inter-country adoption studies are identifying populations of children placed when past infancy. Fanshel's study of American Indian children placed between 1958 and 1967 involved same race and trans-racial placement (Fanshel, 1972). Three hundred and ninety-five children were placed and 97 per cent of these were adopted by white families. The method of evaluation of the placements used was the adoptive parents' accounts of the level of adjustment of the children. More than 50 per cent of the children were described as being relatively problem-free, and another 25 per cent were rated as making an adequate adjustment with strengths outweighing weaknesses. Fanshel also found that the older the child at placement, the less well adjusted was he or she likely to be.

Grow and Shapiro (1975), also in America, reported on the trans-racial placement of 125 black children. They used psychological tests of adjustment in order to measure success, together with interviews with the adoptive parents and the evaluations of teachers. Assessments were also made of the children's attitudes towards race. They concluded that 77 per cent of the children had adjusted successfully. Simon and Altstein (1977 and 1981) reported that approximately 15,000 black or mixed parentage children had been placed trans-racially in the USA before that date, but that the numbers being so placed were greatly diminished because greater efforts were being made to make same-race placements. The 204 children in this study were all placed as babies or toddlers, and were followed-up between the ages of three and eight. One hundred and thirty-three children were followed-up at the age of eleven, again using interviews with parents as the source of evidence. Around 20 per cent of the adoptive parents described problems related either to the adoption of the children or to racial differences. These authors also asked questions about the racial identity of the children but their findings are of limited value given that the source was the parents rather than the children themselves, and no objective measures were used.

Shireman and Johnson (1986) describe a longitudinal study of 118 black children placed for adoption when under the age of three, with single parents, black parents, and white parents. The children were followed up at the ages of 4 and 8, and it is intended that further data will be collected as they grow up. None of the placements had disrupted, but, on the basis of standardised tests, parents' reports, and researchers' observations, the adjustment of 56 of the 71 who agreed to take part was rated as excellent or good (79 per cent). Although those placed transracially still had a good sense of racial identity at the age of eight, the intensity of their black identity had not increased from the age of four to the extent that this had happened for those placed with black families.

14

In Britain Gill and Jackson (1983) have also followed up a group of
black or mixed parentage children placed as babies or toddlers by the
British Adoption project. The families had already been interviewed for
a study by Raynor (1970), between one and four years after placement
when 94 per cent of the children, and 75 per cent of the adoptive
parents were assessed as having made a very good or satisfactory
adjustment to their changed family status. Forty-four of the 51 sets of
parents were interviewed for the Gill and Jackson study when the
children were aged between 12 and 16. Thirty-six were white adopters of
black or mixed parentage children and there were eight couples where at
least one parent was black, thus providing an interesting if small
comparison group. As well as assessing well-being, attention was also
paid to the educational performance of the children, and to their sense
of racial identity, and self-esteem. They found "no evidence that the
experience of racial background had been clearly different" for the two
sets of children (p.131), and 83 per cent of the trans-racial placements
were assessed as being successful. This success rate has been called
into question on the grounds that it gave insufficient weight to the
fact that:

> the large majority of parents had made only limited or very limited
> attempts to give their children a sense of racial pride and
> awareness of their racial origin. The children in turn saw
> themselves as white in all but skin colour and had little knowledge
> or experience of their counterparts growing up in the black
> community (p.130).

Two more extensive studies of trans-racial adoption, in this case
inter-country adoption, are those of Hoksbergen and his colleagues
(1987a and 1987b). The first of these describes an investigation into
the current circumstances of 116 Thai children adopted by Dutch
families. Again the children were mostly babies or toddlers when they
joined their adoptive families. Most were aged between seven and ten at
interview although twelve were over eleven. In some senses this study
is more relevant to our present concern, as many of the children did
indeed have "special needs" since they experienced severe deprivation
before placement or came to their adoptive families with medical
problems, often of a serious nature. It was possible for all the
families who had adopted Thai children to be contacted and a 96 per cent
response rate was obtained. This study is also important because it is
almost a total sample of a large number of adoptive placements. Interviews were obtained with the parents, and behavioural check-lists and
teachers' questionnaires were also used. The findings are similar to
those of Seglow et al. (1972), in that the adopted children were found
to be doing better than the average Dutch child at school. However, as
with the National Child Development Study, and Gill and Jackson's study,
this finding has to be considered alongside the fact that the adoptive
parents tended to live in more advantaged circumstances, and to have
higher educational levels, than parents in the general population.
Well-being was assessed more objectively than is often the case, with
four assessors considering each interview. They concluded that there
were reasons for concern about the child's well-being in 16 per cent of
the families, and they found that those with lower well-being ratings
tended to have been older at the time they were placed, and to have had
problematic backgrounds in their countries of origin. Only 55 per cent
of those who were placed at two years or older were in placements which
were problem-free, compared with 92 per cent of those placed when under
six months of age. These authors also considered the extent to which

15

the children were attached both to their mothers and to their fathers, and conclude that, even with the older children who were presenting behaviour problems, strong attachments had been formed. (Ninety-six per cent of the mothers and 96 per cent of the fathers considered their relationship with the child was either satisfactory or very satisfactory.)

The second study by Hoksbergen and his colleagues (1987b) is of more relevance to this monograph since it involves larger numbers of children placed when older, as well as providing valuable information about inter-country placements. The authors note that 16,000 children from sixteen countries had been adopted in the Netherlands before the 1st January 1986, and that approximately 1,200 children yearly are adopted in this way. This study differs from those previously mentioned in that it identifies for study children where the adoption was not satisfactory. All children admitted on a long or short-term basis to residential care were identified. The authors see this as a valid way into studying unsatisfactory placements since they suggest that adoptive parents are more likely than most to resist placement away from home unless it is absolutely necessary. (As will be seen when we come to discuss services available for special needs adopted children, the use of a stay in residential care as indicating breakdown is debatable.) Since it is possible to identify all the inter-country placements in the Netherlands, and also all those admitted to public care, the authors conclude that on average 2.15 per cent of the inter-country adoptive placements disrupted. The rate for those aged over six at placement was 10.7 per cent. These figures need to be treated with caution, partly because of the definition of disruption and partly because the children had been in placement for varying lengths of time. The age at which children were most likely to need placement away from the home was twelve. The study is particularly interesting because of the detailed accounts of the behaviour of the children which were obtained from the child care workers. Wherever comparable information is available, they compare this behaviour with that of children in similar communities, and also with the group of Thai adopted children already referred to. Although most of these children were black, little attention is paid by this study to the question of racial identity

DISRUPTION STUDIES

Hoksbergen's study of inter-country placements which disrupted leads on to a consideration of those studies which have concentrated on adoptive placements which have not lasted.

In a useful summary article on adoption failure, Kadushin and Seidl (1971) summarise studies of failed adoptive placements involving 34,125 children mostly placed as babies or toddlers, 573 of whom were returned to the agency. The authors then report a study of their own of almost 3,000 children placed between January 1960 and 1967, 2.8 per cent of whom were returned to the agency before being legally adopted. They were able to compare these disrupted placements with those in which adoption was completed, and found a statistically significant relationship between age of the child at placement and the outcome. Whilst only 10 per cent of the children in successful placements were aged 6 years or older at placement, this figure for the failed placements was 30 per cent. They also identified sibling placements as being more likely to disrupt. Twenty-eight per cent of children placed with siblings failed as compared with 1.2 per cent of those placed singly. As the authors point out, this may also be influenced by the fact that more children placed in sibling groups are older at placement. (Hoksbergen (1987b) also found that children placed with siblings were more likely to be admitted to residential care.) As well as being older at placement and being more likely to be placed with siblings, the children whose placements failed studied by Kadushin and Seidl were more likely to have been neglected or to have shown symptoms of deprivation and "would probably come to the adoptive situation with behavioural difficulties and psychic vulnerabilities that are the consequence of developmental trauma, and such behaviour would enhance the risk of placement failure" (p.35). Reasons for failure were identified as belonging to three major groups - those related to situational factors such as financial stress or the death of an adoptive parent; those related to the adoptive parents such as unfulfilled parental expectations, or marital conflict; and those related to the adoptive child such as demanding or anti-social behaviour on the part of the child. Situational factors were identified as being mainly responsible in 22 per cent of cases; problems concerning the child's behaviour in 23.5 per cent of cases, and problems in the adoptive parents or adoptive home in 54.5 per cent of cases.

Most other studies of unsatisfactory adoptions have involved the identification of clinical populations, such as those attending child guidance clinics (Humphrey, 1963; Herbert, 1984; Howe and Hinings, 1987), or being received or committed into care (Howe 1987). Howe and Hinings found that adopted children were marginally over-represented in a population of children referred to a child guidance clinic, and that most of these had been placed as babies. Howe found in respect of adopted children coming into care, mostly as teenagers, that they were no more likely to be in care than non-adopted children in general, but were over-represented if one considers populations of middle class families. Such studies are particularly helpful in describing the types of behavioural or emotional difficulties encountered in samples of adopted children.

Other important sources of information about adopted people are studies of adult adoptees who seek information about their birth families, or actually seek to find them. (See especially Triseliotis, 1973; Haimes and Timms, 1985; Sachdev, 1987). Whilst these are not representative of total populations of adopted adults, they offer qualitative information about some of the concerns of those who "search" and especially about the question of identity and how identity issues were handled as the youngsters grew up. Similar information is also available from accounts written by adopted adults and adoptive parents. (See especially Krementz, 1982).

The work of the Post-Adoption Centre recently established in London by Sawbridge (1988) and to be evaluated by Howe (1988) will provide valuable information on people adopted over periods of years, and also on the sorts of difficulties which they and their adoptive parents experience. In the first year of operation 1,179 people contacted the agency for advice, most of these being adopted adults.

Similar agencies in other parts of the world have evoked interest in the "adoption triangle" or the "adoption circle" (see Sachdev, 1987). In the past, birth parents have only figured in the research literature in terms of their circumstances, and the services offered to them at the time of the adoption. Little is known about their satisfaction with the adoption process in the long-term. In most countries which allow access to adoption records once a young person reaches a given age, birth parents also have rights to information. Experience of such legislation has led some adoption agencies, notably in New Zealand, to re-think the whole question of secrecy in adoption. It is now normal practice in New Zealand for some contact to be maintained between adoptive families and birth parents, even if only by way of occasional letters, or through a third party, and applicants who are totally unwilling to have any form of contact with the birth-parents are not normally accepted as adopters (Corcoran, 1987 and 1988).

To summarise, although most of these adoption studies have been concerned with the placement of babies, some have included children who fall into our "special needs" categories. They have been included in this review of the literature on the success of adoption since a longer term perspective is not yet available for large numbers of special needs placements. They are also relevant to our study in the sense that it is important to ask whether the placement of special needs children does, as has been suggested, differ markedly from the placement of babies. From these studies it would seem that something under 2 per cent of placements break down before adoption is legalised, and it is not known with any certainty what proportion break down before the child reaches adulthood. It seems likely that adopted children are slightly more likely than a population of non-adopted children to experience emotional difficulties as they grow up, but they are likely to do as well at school as comparable populations of children. The few studies which include children placed when past infancy suggest that such placements are more likely to be problematic. The experience is likely to be viewed as satisfactory by something like 80 per cent of the adoptive parents, and of the adopted people but this figure excludes those placements which break down. There seems to be an issue about identity for a minority of adopted people which may impede satisfactory adjustment in adult life. Attempts to identify the sorts of people most likely to suceed as adoptive parents have proved inconclusive.

Whilst such positive findings augur well for a change in policy so that adoption is considered for a wider range of children in care, the almost universal finding that the older the child at placement, the more likely is it that problems will develop, should be noted.

FAMILY PLACEMENT FOR CHILDREN IN LONG-TERM CARE

We have already noted in Chapter 1 that permanence for some children in care will be achieved by placement in a "long-term" or "permanent" foster home. Before moving on to a consideration of studies of the effectiveness of placements made more recently as a result of permanence policies, we need first, therefore, to consider studies which evaluate long-term foster care for "special needs" children. Many of the children described in such studies would, under present policies, have been placed for adoption. However, adoption has not until recently been considered an option for the majority of children in care for three reasons. First, so long as there were large numbers of healthy white babies available for placement, it was assumed by most adoption workers that families would be unlikely to offer to adopt those who came into the special needs categories. Secondly, the corollary of this was that it was considered that only children with a clean bill of mental and physical health should be placed for adoption. The third reason was that it was not usually considered appropriate to place children for adoption against their parents' wishes, and indeed it was difficult to do so until a shift in opinion about the relative weight to be placed on children's rights and parents' rights led to the 1975 Children Act and a changing view amongst the judiciary about what constitutes the "unreasonably withholding" of consent to adoption.

We saw in Chapter 1 that the emphasis on prevention in the 1960s and early 1970s meant that it was unusual for it to be formally accepted that a youngster would remain in care until he or she grew up, so that few foster children and foster parents were offered the security of knowing that they would remain together as a family. We hypothesised that these policies might have contributed to some extent to the high breakdown rate (around 50 per cent within 5 years of placement) of long-term foster placements reported by Trasler (1960), Parker (1966), and George (1970).

Studies of long-term foster care (most recently reviewed by Shaw, 1987) have used very different definitions of "long-term", and it is difficult to identify research studies of long-term foster care which was intended to provide a home for the youngster until adulthood, since it was rare for such a decision to be made explicit. The situation is complicated by the fact that in America foster care also includes children in what in Britain would be described as children's homes.

Turning explicity to measures of success, most of the earlier studies used the unplanned removal of the child from the home as an indicator of success or otherwise. Other studies have defined effectiveness in terms of the well-being of the children, and have usually included a consideration of the children's sense of identity. The most important of these studies is that conducted by Fanshel and Shinn (1978) into the care careers of 624 children in New York State. This was a longitudinal study which followed the children for a 5-year period after they came into care in 1966. The children were assessed three times during the five-year period. Nearly 5 per cent left care through adoption and 36 per cent were still in care at the end of the study. The authors report on the well-being of the children, through their own, and their social workers' eyes, and also utilise a battery of tests of health, educational progress and other indicators. Although providing the most comprehensive material available about the behaviour and functioning of a large group of children placed away from home, the complexity of the sample does not allow for firm conclusions to be drawn about the effectiveness of long-term substitute family placements. One of the important findings was that the well-being of children in long-term care tends to be higher and the rating by teachers to be more positive if they remain in contact with natural parents. The researchers concluded that between 25 and 33 per cent of the children in long-term care showed signs of emotional impairment, and although a comparison group was not built into the study, they cited a similar study of children "in welfare families" where 36 per cent had moderate or worse ratings in developmental impairment, and 20 per cent had serious behaviour difficulties. Those researchers concluded that "our findings do not show that children who remained in foster care fared less well with respect to intellectual abilities, school performance, and personal and social adjustment compared to those who returned to their own homes." However, clearly somewhat surprised by this conclusion, they add "we are not sure that our procedures have captured the potential feelings of pain and impaired self-image that can be created by impermanent status in foster care" (p.479).

Another American study by Festinger (1983) of 277 young adults who had mostly been brought up in stable foster homes resulted in a similar conclusion. "The assumptions and expectations that abound concerning the dire fate of foster care children seem to have little validity" (p.293).

The Oregon Project (Lahti et al., 1982) reports findings from a demonstration project aiming to provide permanent homes for 259 children in long-term care. Twenty-six per cent of these returned home and 20 per cent (102) were adopted by strangers. A further 20 per cent (102) were adopted by the existing foster parents and 34 per cent were still in foster care. These researchers also did not find the expected difference in adjustment between the children in temporary foster care and those in permanent placements.

Proch (1982) reports interviews with 29 children aged between 7 and 13 who had been adopted by their foster parents, and with 56 adoptive parents whose children were originally placed as foster children. Although adopted late, over two-thirds had been placed before the age of two years. Few of the adoptive parents defined the foster parent role as temporary, and only 8 of the 29 children could distinguish between foster care and adoption. "The critical element appears to be the child's placement history - the act of adoption was significant if the child had had multiple placements. It was not significant if the child was adopted by the only parents he or she could remember" (p.266).

In an important article summarising findings from 12 studies of children growing up in foster care Maluccio and Fein (1985) comment that despite:

> widespread perception that placement in foster care has short-term as well as long-term adverse effects on children ... researchers have consistently reported that foster care graduates function well, or that no negative effect of foster care on the child's adjustment is detected (p.25).

British studies of children in foster care find higher rates of disturbance, (although comparison groups are rarely available), as well as high breakdown rates. Jenkins (1969) found that 57 per cent of children who had been in foster homes for over 18-months showed poor emotional adjustment. Thorpe (1980) studied 121 foster children aged between 5 and 17 when placed who had been in placement for at least 12-months. Using the Rutter adjustment scale (Rutter et al., 1975), she assessed that 39 per cent showed evidence of disturbance (as compared with 7 per cent of children in a general population living in the Isle of Wight, and 25 per cent of boys and 13 per cent of girls living in Inner London). She noted that children were less likely to be disturbed if they had a good knowledge and understanding of their situation and of the agency, and that such understanding was related to contact with the natural family.

As part of their study of children placed for adoption when aged between two and ten, Triseliotis (1980) and Triseliotis and Russell (1984) collected material on 40 young adults who had grown up in foster care. Whilst the satisfaction ratings for parents and children were lower than for those who had been adopted, Triseliotis places 60 per cent in a "successful" category, and a further 15 per cent are described as being generally satisfied with growing up in foster care, but experiencing some difficulties.

In the course of a more recent study of the payment of adoption allowances to enable children to be adopted by their long-term foster parents, Triseliotis and Hill (1987) interviewed nine children in different families about their experience and perception of changing from foster to adoptive status. Whilst most reported feeling secure and wanted by their foster parents before adoption, they welcomed the change of status for immediate practical benefits such as being able to have the same name as the family, no longer having to be visited by a social worker, or have annual medicals, and for more symbolic reasons which implied "being really their child" and "a proper part of the family."

The major study of well-being of long-term foster children, in this case all in placement for at least five years, is that of Rowe and her colleagues (1984). They also used the Rutter scale, alongside interviews with foster parents and children and with a small group of natural parents. The majority of these youngsters had been placed when under five and one might therefore have expected similar positive scores of well-being as one would find in a population of adopted children. However, this was not the case, with quite high disturbance rates being noted (30 per cent, compared with 11 per cent of those adopted by foster parents). Echoing Bohman's (1980) tentative explanation for a higher rate of maladjustment amongst children brought up in foster care, Rowe and her colleagues hypothesised that this might in part be accounted for by the sense of insecurity of which some of the foster parents and children spoke. Lahti (1982) notes from the study just mentioned that well-being is positively related to a _sense_ of permanence, which is not necessarily the same as _legal_ permanence.

Since they were only looking at children who remained in placement, Rowe's and Triseliotis' studies were unable to provide information about breakdown rates. However, Berridge and Cleaver's 1987 book on foster home breakdown provides valuable up-to-date information. These authors identified populations of children in planned long-term foster care in two Social Services Departments and a voluntary agency. They found that 42 per cent of children fostered with strangers experienced breakdown within three years in the county authority, whereas only 21 per cent of the London borough placements broke down within three years. They identified reasons for breakdown in terms of child focussed problems (62 per cent of cases); natural parent focussed problems (present in 8 per cent of cases); and placement focussed problems, that is those which emanated primarily from the foster household (present in 73 per cent of cases). Unlike the studies of children placed for adoption to which we have already referred, almost a half of these children were aged 6 or over at the time of placement. Those who were older when placed were more likely to experience breakdown, but the differences were not statistically significant. On the other hand, a finding which is in contradiction to some of the adoption studies, is that children placed singly, away from siblings living elsewhere, were more likely to experience breakdown than children placed together with siblings. Berridge and Cleaver's study supports those of Parker and Trasler in its finding that breakdown is more likely to occur if there is a natural child of the family who is either younger or of about the same age as the foster child. They also find that placements of children who have been long in care are more vulnerable to breakdown.

In a more recent study, Rowe and her colleagues (1988) studied the outcomes of over 3,000 foster care placements which ended either because the child went out of care at 18 or for other planned or unplanned reasons. Twenty-four per cent of those foster placements had not lasted as long as needed. This study used as a crude measure of "success" whether or not a placement lasted as needed, and also achieved placement aims. On this basis, success rates for foster home outcomes ranged from 56.6 in one authority to 68.6 in another. Three hundred and forty-five of the foster placements studied had lasted at least three years, but 22 per cent of these had not lasted as long as needed, and a further 10 per cent were said to have lasted too long (an interesting measure of outcome not found in other studies). Twenty-seven per cent of the 199 long-term placements made in the first year had broken down by the end of the second year of the study, the proportion increasing with age at placement, but the authors stress that this rate of breakdown should be viewed in the light of the serious problems and older age range of these children, than groups studied in the 60s.

A distinction should be made here between long-term foster placements, and foster placements with a view to adoption (which were not included in Berridge and Cleaver's 1987 study). These latter approximate most closely to what we will subsequently examine as permanent foster placements in that the foster parents and children might be expected to have a greater sense of permanence. There are no British studies specifically of fostering with a view to adoption. Some such families are included amongst those studied by Rowe et al. (1984), who eventually adopted the children in their care, although others amongst this group adopted children who were originally intended to be short-stay. Proportionately more of the children remaining in short-stay placements which became adoptions, and those fostered with a view to adoption where the children were eventually adopted, were rated by the researchers as doing well than of those in long-term foster placements. However, this may well be because the children were younger at placement, or because families were more likely to proceed to adoption if the placement was already perceived as satisfactory. Of the 345 long-term foster placement endings in Rowe et al's 1988 study, 62 children were being adopted by their foster parents.

American permanent placement studies usually include as adoptive placements those adopted by foster parents with whom they were already living, although some studies also distinguish between groups of children adopted by foster parents and those adopted by families who were new to them. (As we shall see, it is the inclusion of these placements which largely accounts for American disruption rates being lower than English ones). Fein et al (1983) found that 7 per cent of the 187 children placed permanently were adopted by the foster families with whom they were already living, and noted that foster parent adoptive homes along with placement with relatives, had higher adjustment scores. In the study by Lahti (1982) 20 per cent had been adopted by their existing foster parents. They report that some 15-months after placement 93 per cent of those adopted by foster parents were still there (compared with 100 per cent of those adopted by strangers) but that the well-being score of those adopted by their foster parents was higher than those adopted by strangers.

22

Festinger (1986) studied in some detail 183 children who were at least six when applications to adopt were made and whose average age at placement was four. This somewhat complex, and at times confusing, comparison between children whose placements disrupted and those who remained in placement for 12-24 months, involved 70 per cent of children whose existing foster parents applied to adopt them. The author concludes that such placements were less likely to disrupt than placements with new families. However, since, by definition, those foster placements which disrupted without an application to adopt are excluded, this study does not give a disruption rate for long-term foster care.

In Britain Raynor (1980) included 56 children who had first been placed as foster children when she studied the adjustment of young adults who had been adopted. All were placed as babies or toddlers, but some were not adopted by their foster parents until five years after placement. She found no significant difference in adjustment between these children and those placed directly for adoption. (Seventy-one per cent of the early adopted children were of excellent or good adjustment compared with 68 per cent of those adopted by their foster parents).

The proportion of children leaving care through adoption in Britain has increased from 3.9 per cent in 1979 to 5.6 percent in 1984. Howe (1984) shows that out of all adoption orders made in 1984, 31 per cent were for children of school age. These placements were mostly made some years ago before agencies became committed to permanence policies and started to place directly with families intending to apply for adoption. Most are therefore likely to have been long-term foster children placed as infants and adopted by their foster parents at school age when they were already well settled.

It might be expected that children in long-term care would still be in regular contact with members of their birth families, but several studies have indicated that this is unlikely to be the case, once children have been in care for more than a few months. (See especially Millham et al., 1986). However, as Triseliotis (1986) has pointed out, the more quickly agencies move towards making permanency plans for children in their care, the more children will there be who are still in contact with birth families.

To summmarise, the majority of children in long-term care will be either moving between foster homes which disrupt and residential placements, or be in foster placements which were initially intended to be short-term and have become long-term. They are likely to have lost touch with members of their birth families, and yet the placement will be unlikely to offer them a sense of permanence since social work practice will be geared to a fostering status and regulations which imply impermanence. A smaller number will be fostered with a view to adoption and some research studies show that if they settle in successfully these are likely to be amongst the more successful foster care placements, perhaps because of the greater clarity of purpose. The numbers fostered with a view to adoption at any one time are likely to decrease, as foster parents are encouraged to adopt more quickly, if necessary with the help of adoption allowances. Studies of foster care, like those of adoption, are inconclusive about the sorts of families most likely to be successful, other than in their finding that families with a child near in age to the foster child are more likely to break down. Most also conclude that those placed with older parents are less likely to experience foster home breakdown. Whilst it is generally held that prolonged stays in foster care have a negative effect on well-being, research studies offer conflicting evidence on this point.

3 Research into permanent family placement for children with 'special needs'

Although some of the adoption studies already described included some "special needs" children, such placements were made before the introduction of new policies and practices specifically geared to the needs of this group. (See Chapter 1 for a discussion of the term "special needs"). The first reports to appear were essentially descriptive, although they did give some information about placements which disrupted (see especially Donley 1975; Jewett 1978; Sawbridge, 1980; Lindsay-Smith and Price, 1980; Fitzgerald et al., 1982; Fratter et al., 1982). The first British independent, though in-house, study was of the Barnardo's New Families' Project (Kerrane, et al., 1981). Independent evaluative studies have more recently been published, both in America and Britain. Barth et al. (1986) and Barth and Berry (1987) offer important summaries of the research into outcomes of a range of permanent family placements, including placements back with birth families. These authors consider four different measures of outcome - whether the child was re-abused; whether the placement lasted; developmental outcomes for the children; and children's satisfaction. Reid and his colleagues (1987), Katz (1986), and Seltzer and Bloksberg (1987) also summarise findings in respect of the placement of older youngsters experiencing behaviour difficulties and identify some of the characteristics of the youngsters and of the new families which have been associated with success in the various studies. These tend to be personal characteristics of the parents rather than concrete factors such as age, or whether they have children of their own.

Some of the studies are large-scale surveys which usually use continuation in placement as the measure of success. Some also include assessments of the well-being of the children and accounts of the satisfaction of the parents, and sometimes of the children. Other studies, mostly small-scale and retrospective, take a population of children and families and aim to identify factors associated with the more successful placements, or with disruptions. One or two retrospective studies have involved larger numbers, the researchers looking back over populations of children placed, mainly to ascertain whether the placements survived or disrupted, and to consider whether any particular factors in children or new parents are associated with either outcome. The number of prospective studies of permanent placement of special needs children is still small, and such studies usually involve small numbers, and follow the children through for comparatively brief periods of time. Some consider disruption or otherwise as a measure of success, whilst others also interview parents and children citing satisfaction levels as measures of success, and sometimes also an overall rating of well-being.

We shall consider these studies in terms of the measures of success used - firstly, those which provide information about breakdown rates, and factors associated with breakdown; secondly, those which assess the well-being of children still in placement; and, thirdly, those very few studies and other sources of information which tell us something of the children who have been assessed as needing permanent family placement, but who have not been placed. Unless otherwise stated, the research cited will be that which is relevant to general populations of "special needs" children in care, as opposed to more strictly defined groups such as handicapped babies.

STUDIES OF BREAKDOWN RATES

One might expect that the major sources of information about breakdown rates in special needs family placements would come from America since that country has been involved in such work for longer. There are, indeed, several accounts - including statistical studies from the different placing agencies, and independent evaluations of the work of the demonstration projects which had an evaluation element built into them (Stein et al., 1978; Lahti, 1982; Fein et al., 1983). A weakness of these studies is that timescales at follow-up tend to be short. Nevertheless, they show a high success rate, all the 52 children adopted by strangers in Lahti's study being still in placement 15-months later.

Fein et al. summarise those studies which have attempted to follow up children in permanent placement. Unfortunately for our purposes, they tend not to differentiate between children being "permanently" placed back with natural parents, remaining on a permanent basis with their foster parents, or being placed for adoption or permanent fostering with strangers. These authors then identify 726 children placed permanently in New York State, and it is possible to identify 93 of these who were adopted by strangers. One hundred and eighty-seven of these children, including 63 who were adopted or permanently fostered are described in more detail. Only one of the adoptive placements had broken down one year after placement, but caution is needed in interpreting this as a disruption rate since there is no way of knowing what happened to the children originally placed in this way but not included in the sample. The placements of half of those who were permanently fostered (mostly older children) had disrupted. One year is also a very early stage at which to assess breakdown.

Festinger (1986), in the only book which specifically sets out to explore the subject of disruption in special needs placements, (mainly older children in care), uses a very narrow definition of disruption. She does not include those placements which broke down after adoption, but does include amongst the disruptions those cases where foster parents applied to adopt, and did not go through with the application, although the child remained with them. (In terms of our definition of permanent family placement in Chapter 1, this would certainly not be seen as a disruption, since the child remained in permanent placement.) She also includes those cases where children already well settled in their foster homes were adopted by their foster parents and where there is a higher chance of success as parents and child are likely to have already become attached. The study had a somewhat complex "wrap-around" design which eventually identified 482 children in respect of whom adoption agreements were signed, and followed them through for a 12-month period. Festinger estimated that "8.2 per cent of all the adoptive placements disrupted, 1.3 per cent of the placements changed from adoptive status to on-going foster care in the same home, 46.2 per cent of the children were adopted, and the outcome of the remaining 44.3 per cent was not yet known. The last group continues to remain on adoptive status in the same homes that had signed adoption agreements 12-months earlier" (Festinger, 1986, p.11). Some of those not yet adopted at the 12-month stage were followed through and on the basis of these findings Festinger concludes that the overall disruption rate was somewhere between 12 and 14 per cent. It proved not possible to distinguish between those placements which were with new families and those where existing foster parents applied to adopt. Like other researchers she noted a high disruption rate amongst older children and estimated that between 15 and 17 per cent of those aged over eleven when the adoption agreement was signed disrupted. (These may well have been younger when placed with their foster families.) She also found that children placed alone were significantly more likely to disrupt (11.7 per cent) than those placed with siblings (6 per cent).

Festinger then describes a study in which 56 children adopted singly were compared with 53 disruptions of single child placements and four children who remained in the home but were not adopted. She also considers children placed as sibling groups, and thus compares a total of 78 children whose placements disrupted with 105 who were adopted. Thirty-one per cent of the placements studied were with new families, and are therefore directly relevant to our study. Placements with new families were more vulnerable to disruption (53 per cent of those which disrupted were placements with new families compared with 15 per cent of the placements which did not disrupt). The sample includes all placements which disrupted, but only a random sample of those which did not, and it is therefore not possible to say what proportion of placements with strangers disrupted compared with adoptions by existing foster parents. In the total sample:

all along, at entry or freeing and especially at agreement, age was a predicter of outcome ... it is also quite possible that because of their older age more had developed firmer psychological links to their families of origin, and may even have viewed adoption as an act of disloyalty (p.24).

This higher disruption rate for older children was present amongst the sibling groups as well as amongst those placed singly. In looking at the siblings, Festinger, like Berridge and Cleaver (1987), albeit with different definitions, finds that "children whose placements disrupted were more likely to have siblings living elsewhere (20.8 per cent) than those who were adopted (3.6 per cent)" (p.25).

Festinger also considers characteristics of the adoptive parents. Interestingly, a majority of the children were placed for adoption with black families, and only 5 per cent were placed across racial lines. Like other researchers, Festinger was unable clearly to identify characteristics of the new families which were related to disruption, although the descriptive material provides some fascinating information. She concludes that:

> in sum most aspects of these households - the number of older children, their ages, sex, and race - were not related to the outcome. Elements that distinguish between disruptions and adoptions such as the middle position in age or the lone position with regard to sex, were few in number. They do not form a common thread, are difficult to explain, and indeed may be due to chance (p.31).

Finally, Festinger considers factors related to the background of the children and their attachments with important people from the past. Those who experienced disruption were likely to be older at the time they last saw their birth parents than those who were adopted:

> This is in line with their older age all along and lends further support to the notion that more of those whose placements disrupted had developed firmer psychological links to their families of origin than youngsters who were adopted. This, rather than the recency of their contacts, appeared to be important, for recency was immaterial to the outcome. For example, less than two years had elapsed between the most recent contact with biological parents and the signing of adoption agreements for roughly the same proportion of disruption (43.4 per cent) and of adoption (40.2 per cent) outcomes.

> Furthermore, children who maintained contact with someone who was thought to be opposed to their adoption were more apt to be in a placement that disrupted than one in which they were adopted. Roughly 12 per cent of the children maintained such a relationship, usually with a biological parent or older sibling, but the proportion was higher amongst those whose placement disrupted (21.2 per cent) than amongst the adoptees (4.9 per cent) (pp.33-34).

This study by Festinger has been summarised at greater length because, despite its complexity and the limitations arising from the way in which the statistics are presented, it is the most comprehensive study to date of disruption amongst placements of special needs children. The reasons for disruption most frequently identified are listed as:

- the unrealistic expectations of the families and problems in coping with the children (56.4 per cent)

- the children's own expectations were not fulfilled or their own style of living was not really accepted (20.5 per cent)

- problems in the motivation of the substitute families (19.2 per cent)

28

- environmental influences on the children such as a pull on the   child from members of birth family or former foster parents (15.4 per cent)

- marital difficulties (11.5 per cent)

- problems in the motivation of the children themselves (11.5 per cent)

- environmental stresses on the substitute family, for example, a death in the extended family or a serious problem for a child of the family or opposition to the adoption by family members living elsewhere (10.3 per cent)

- the needs of the child and the substitute family did not mesh (9 per cent)

- physical illness of an adoptive parent (5.1 per cent)

- allegations of parental misconduct (3.8 per cent).

The author concludes:

> It is clear that by far the most important element cited by case workers concerned family expectations and their ability or willingness to cope with the children's demands and behaviours. When one adds the cases where children's expectations were an issue and those where needs did not mesh, one can see that more than half of the cases showed a kind of mis-match, in the sense that the chemistry appeared to be wrong, or soured after a time. It is also possible that some of these families misjudged their own abilities or were encouraged to adopt children who were really more than they could handle (p.40).

Another American study which includes an assessment of breakdown is that of Nelson (1985). Adoptive families of special needs children were followed-up between one and four years after the adoption order was made, which might have been considerably later than the original placement. A response rate of 47 per cent of the 373 eligible families was obtained and the study therefore concerned 177 families (257 children), 99 of whom were new families as compared with 73 foster parent adopters. Outcome was measured in terms of the quality of the children's lives, and parental satisfaction with adoption, as well as breakdowns. In only 3 per cent of cases (seven children adopted by five families) had the children left the placements permanently, although with a response rate of only 47 per cent this finding must be treated with caution. A further nine children from 12 families had left home for periods of time because of problems experienced by either the child or the parent. Six of the seven cases where disruption occurred were those where the placement had been with a new family.

Further American information about disruption rates comes from Hornby (1986) and Kaye (1985). Hornby reports on a study of over 200 adoptive families, a quarter of which had experienced disruption. This was not a random sample but the authors elsewhere in the article, describing children with special needs placed for adoption in Southern Maine, reported that 10 per cent of adoptions disrupted within the first three years of placement. ("Disruption" for this author includes placements which terminated both before and after legal adoption.) Characteristics of the children associated with disruption were: a history of physical, sexual or emotional abuse; and difficult behaviour, especially if it involved eating disorders, sexual promiscuity, suicidal behaviour, fire-starting, stealing, or vandalism. In terms of the families, the author concludes:

> our case record analysis shows that married couples as opposed to single parents, families with prior adoptive experience, white parents and couples where both partners have an equal commitment to the adoption, experience significantly fewer disruptions. Size of family, age of the parent, income, fertility history and educational background are not associated one way or another with disruption. Similarly, trans-racial placements appear as likely to succeed as same-race adoptions (p.9).

Detailed interviews revealed less concrete but nonetheless valuable information, such as the conclusion that "parents have a better chance if they can take some credit for the improvements their children make, but little blame for their failures."

There are several interesting conclusions about the nature of the social work service offered. About two-thirds of the families requested help before disruption:

> When agencies do sense difficulties, their most prevalent response is to increase caseworker time with the family and/or the child. In addition, referrals to counselling or therapy are made in nearly half the cases. Few attempted trial separations. Whilst several parents begged for the child to be placed in residential treatment for a period of time, the agencies with the responsibility to pay are often reluctant due to the cost and the fear that the child will never return (p.11).

This conclusion is interesting in the light of Nelson's finding that placement away from home was a much valued method of help to adoptive families. It is also a useful reminder that adoptive families and "natural families" react very similarly and have similar problems in getting their views about the need for breathing space across to social workers. (See especially Packman, 1986; Fisher et al., 1986). We return to this issue in the concluding chapter.

Kaye and Tipton (1985) report on a major investigation on behalf of the American Office of Health Development Services. Defining disruption as the termination of placements before legal adoption, they came to the conclusion that there was a 13 per cent disruption rate. More disruptions occured for children with emotional problems, and physically and mentally handicapped children were less likely to be involved in disruption. Reasons for disruption were the child's behaviour, lack of bonding, and the child's inability to meet parental expectation. The information on which these conclusions are based was obtained from five American States, and surprisingly similar conclusions were reached, especially about higher disruption rates for those who were older at placement. On the other hand, in this study siblings placed together were more likely to be over-represented amongst children whose placements disrupted. Less traditional adopters were as successful as those more usually considered as suitable to adopt. Parents over 40 were less likely to be involved in disruptions, as were parents from minority ethnic groups and those in lower income brackets. Single parents were equally represented in both groups.

Kagan and Reid (1986) consider the progress of 78 young people whose average age was 11 at the time of placement five years after they joined their adoptive families. All had emotional and behavioural difficulties as well as being older, and success was measured in terms of well-being as well as whether the placement disrupted and whether the young person was adopted. Seventy-one per cent of the youngsters were adopted, and 53 per cent lived with the new family for five years or until the age of 18. Thirteen per cent of those who had been adopted experienced disruption. Amongst factors identfied as being associated with a positive outcome was placement with a sibling, a finding of other studies reviewed here. The authors note that quality of social work service varied, but were unable to quantify this and include it as a variable.

Fein and her colleagues (1979) compared 13 latency age children with behaviour disturbances who were placed for adoption, with 12 similar children who returned home, and found a similar breakdown rate (69 per cent and 67 per cent) for each group. The possible length of time in placement at follow up varied between a few months and five years.

Coyne and Brown (1985) evaluated the placement for adoption of 693 "developmentally disabled" children, almost half of whom were of school age when placed, and 26 per cent of whom were "claimed" by their foster parents. Just under 9 per cent of these had disrupted within one year of placement, and disruption was more likely to occur when children were over seven at placement (18 per cent disrupted) and less likely when children were adopted by their foster parents. Profoundly handicapped children were less likely to experience disruption than those with moderate handicaps.

In Britain the major source of information to date about disruptions comes from specialist placement agencies mainly in the voluntary sector. All are placing special needs children, and although most are adoption agencies, some of the children will remain in permanent foster placement either through design or because the moment to adopt never seems right. The term disruption therefore is used here to mean removal of the child from placement, either before or after legal adoption. Until recently the main source of information about disruptions was the Annual Reports of these agencies (see especially the Annual Reports of Parents for Children which showed that, by 1986, 89 children had been placed and 15 per cent of these placements had disrupted). A more extensive survey is currently being undertaken by Thoburn and Rowe (1988), which indicates that 1,165 children with special needs were placed by the voluntary agencies between 1980 and the end of 1984. (See Table 1 for details about characteristics of the children and their special needs.) Table 2 shows that the average disruption rate within eighteen months to six years of placement was at least 22 per cent. (Eventual outcomes for some of the earlier placed children with whom the agencies were no longer in contact were not known.) The study confirms findings from America that age at placement is significantly related to disruption, but the overall disruption rate is considerably higher than that cited by American studies. This is almost certainly explained by the fact that all these placements were with new families, and existing foster placements which became permanent were omitted. In this overall average, disruption rates varied from 0 per cent to 96 per cent for the individual agencies - this variation being mainly accounted for by the age at placement of the youngsters, some agencies specialising in the adoptive placement of handicapped babies, where as we shall see the disruption rate is considerably lower. This survey confirms the findings of most other studies that older age at placement is related to less favourable outcomes. Seventeen per cent of those placed at age 5-8 experienced breakdowns compared to 32 per cent of those placed between the ages of 9 and 11. Children who were older at placement were less likely to be adopted, and more likely to be in permanent foster homes.

Table 2
Disruption and adoption rates amongst children
placed by British voluntary agencies 1980-84
(percentages)

| Status 18 months - 5 years after placement | Age at placement | | | | | | Total % |
	0-2	3-4	5-8	9-11	12-14	15+	
Adopted (or application lodged)	90	84	64	42	21	24	58
Fostered with view to adoption	3	4	9	8	5	3)	
						)	18
Permanently fostered	3	5	10	18	33	35)	
Disrupted	3	7	17	32	40	38	22
Other (e.g. died, returned to birth parents)							2
Total %	100	100	100	100	100	100	100
Total No.	201	127	372	253	178	34	1,165

The largest detailed research project which includes information about disruptions is that of Wolkind and Kozaruk (1983 and 1986). They identified 108 children with medical and developmental problems placed for adoption through the Adoption Resource Exchange between 1974 and 1977. Twenty-three agencies were involved and at the stage of contact just under 5 per cent of the placements had broken down. The children were aged between 3-months and 11 years at placement, but most were babies or toddlers - the average age being three years. Seven families refused to participate and 12 could not be traced - the authors noted that the characteristics of the refusers and those whose placements had broken down were very similar. The children whose placements were least successful tended to be over five at placement, to have had over two years in residential care before placement, to be white, and to have a degree of mental retardation.

Fratter et al. (1982), in an "in-house" account of the Barnardo's Cambridge Cottage Unit, describe their work in placing 42 children in either adoptive or permanent foster homes. The average age of these children was considerably higher than those in Wolkind's study (7 years, 10 months) and 12 per cent of the placements had disrupted at the end of the study.

Kerrane et al. (1982) found that 73 children were placed during the first four years of the Barnardo's New Families Glasgow project, and that nine of those had broken down (12 per cent), though some of the later placed would have been in placement for a very short period of time, so that the overall "disruption rate" is likely to be higher. Six of those nine were aged 10 to 14 at placement.

Hart (1986), in a study of the work of the Manchester Adoption Society, found that 92 of the 172 children referred were placed over a five year period. He studied 60 of these children, mostly over five or members of sibling groups, and found that 5 per cent broke down by the end of the study (between one and five years since placement).

One hundred and sixty children in care who were members of sibling groups were studied by Wedge and Mantle (1988). Most of the 133 who were placed with permanent new adoptive or foster families remained with at least one sibling. Nine months to four years after placement, 21 per cent of the children had experienced breakdown. Children placed with a sibling were neither more nor less likely to experience breakdown than those separated from a sibling, but the authors urge caution since the numbers placed separately from siblings are small.

Local authorities are increasingly making their own permanent placements, and systematic accounts of their work are beginning to appear. Wedge (1986) describes the work of the Essex Specialist Family Placement Service which was provided jointly with Barnardo's. He estimated that approximately one in five of the 94 children placed had left their placements two-and-a-half years into the life of the Units. In our study of the work of the "Child Wants A Home" project in Norwich, to which we shall return in Chapter 4, only one of the 22 placements had disrupted within two years, a breakdown rate of 5 per cent.

Rowe and her colleagues (1988) in a study of the children in care in six English local authorities found that "infant adoptions were surprisingly numerous, adoption placements of older or handicapped children were fewer than we had expected, and only six custodianship orders were made during the two years of the project." There were only 40 placements of school age children where the aim was "adoption by this family." Of the 21 children aged five or older placed in the first year of the study, seven had broken down during the period of 13 to 23 months after placement.

O'Hara and Hoggan (1988), evaluating the success of the Lothian home-finding teams in finding permanent adoptive or foster families for "special needs" children in care, found a disruption rate of 4.6 per cent for those who were under 10 at placement, and 21.7 per cent for those aged 10 or over. Disruptions were defined as placements which ceased before the age of 16 (the age of majority in Scotland). The 335 placements studied were made anything between a few months to five years before the date of evaluation, and 10 per cent of the children were "claimed" by existing foster parents. The inclusion of these "claimed" children may partially explain a breakdown rate lower than that of other British studies, although other explanations may lie in the fact that all the preparation work with the children, as well as the preparation of new families and their support after placement, is undertaken by specialist workers with small caseloads. It is also of interest that adoption allowances were paid in respect of 29 per cent of these children (see Triseliotis and Hill, 1988, for an account of the adoption allowance scheme in Scotland.)

From these research reports, one can see that it would be fool-hardy to give a simple breakdown rate for the placement of children with special needs with new families. So much depends on the sort of children being placed, and especially the age at placement, the definition of breakdown, and the time since placement at which any assessment is made.

STUDIES ASSESSING SATISFACTION OF PARENTS AND CHILDREN, AND CHILDREN'S WELL-BEING

Apart from the large-scale surveys, most of the studies already mentioned have considered the satisfaction of parents and/or children with the placement, and attempted to assess well-being. The most important American study in this respect is that of Nelson (1985) whose sample of 177 families had adopted 257 children whose "special needs" were defined similarly to those in Table 1. Information about well-being was collected from interviews with the child's primary caretaker, usually the mother, from a postal questionnaire, and from reading of the files. According to the parents, 85 per cent of the children developed a sense of permanence and 85 per cent of the parents reported that the child improved in regard to school work, or health, or ability to make good relationships. Parental satisfaction, as assessed by the interviewer in the light of the parents' comments, was excellent or good in 73 per cent of cases, and satisfactory in 20 per cent of cases. The major part of the study is made up of detailed accounts of the services available to the families.

The major independent studies of special needs placement in Britain are summarised by Wedge and Thoburn (1987) and Rushton and Treseder (1986). Most studies used a variety of measures of well-being, as well as assessing satisfaction. Most researchers undertook lengthy interviews with the families and were able to use their own observations of relationships between parents and children:

> Our observations of the family during the two hours or more spent on the interview, combined with the cross-checking nature of our inter-viewing techniques, allowed us to feel that we could be reasonably confident of the quality of our data. In only five cases (6 per cent) had things turned out worse or more difficult than expected

34

and in only one of these was the disappointment such that there were real doubts and regrets about the adoption. For the remaining 94 per cent approximately half felt that things had turned out much as they anticipated and the remainder felt that they had turned out better (Wolkind and Kozaruk, p.19).

Macaskill (1985a and 1988) followed up 20 adoptive families and their 23 mentally handicapped adopted children, and found similarly positive results. The children had been in placement from between six months and over four years when first assessed and 17 families were visited again six years later. Interviews were arranged with adoptive parents, with siblings who were old enough, and with the social workers. She concludes, in respect of the siblings, that "contrary to expectations, there was little evidence of the handicapped child destroying family life or adversely affecting siblings." For the 1988 study, 28 children were considered as some families had adopted other children who had disabilities. One of the earlier placements had disrupted, but the other 23, although not without problems, especially for those placed when older, were described as progressing satisfactorily. The author notes that in the later years of placement respite care was increasingly used and valued. These studies are essentially descriptive, but lend weight to Wolkind and Kozaruk's finding that the majority of adoptive parents of handicapped children derive considerable satisfaction from their undertaking.

In another descriptive study, this time of 37 of the more complex placements made by "Parents for Children" between 18 months and 6 years before the interview, Macaskill (1985b) finds a more complex picture. Twenty-one of the children had been adopted by the time of her interview with the families, and one of her interesting conclusions is that the confidence of adoption workers that adoption itself will help to alleviate problems is rarely justified:

A widely held opinion was that the security of adoption would reduce difficulties in problematic placements; the ensuing histories of children were searched in vain for any evidence to validate this belief. The more common reaction was a temporary lull in the onslaught of behavioural difficulties for a few months before and after adoption. ... as the formality of the adoption process receded into past history leaving the same accumulation of problems, hope began to wane and problems took on rather a different perspective (p.41).

She found that the third year of placement was a particularly vulnerable period, an important finding for researchers and practitioners alike, since few research studies have followed children through beyond this period of time. However, even with a sample which was collected because of the degree of complexity of the placement, 13 of the 24 placements which extended beyond two years were characterised by mutually rewarding relationships between parents and children. Even at this stage the children were by no means "cured":

It was noticeable, however, that even in the most settled and successful placements children seemed to retain a certain vulnerability. Problems which had been acutely obvious during the early stages of placement seemed only to be lying dormant, and any crisis or unexpected disturbance of the child's regular routine could quickly reactivate old behaviour patterns (p.43).

The most extensive study of Parents for Children was conducted by the National Children's Bureau, (1986) and Reich and Lewis, (1986). Assessments of success were made in terms of the overall appropriateness of the placement; the child's adaptation to the family; the parents' adaptation to the child; overall assessment of the child's adjustment; rating of the adoptive home; and likelihood of disruption. Ratings were made by the research team, the "Parents for Children" team, and the referring social workers. Over 80 per cent of the placements were rated by all three groups as either very appropriate, or appropriate. In 70 per cent the children's adaptation to the family was excellent or good, and 60 per cent of the parents were described as having made an excellent or good adaptation to the child. Eighty per cent of all placements were regarded as stable with little possibility of disruption.

Our longitudinal study of 21 children placed with permanent new adoptive or foster families by the Children's Society (Thoburn et al., 1987) involved interviews with children, new parents and social workers three times during the first two years. Our conclusions are similar to those of the other studies, but more information is available on the other members of the adoptive or foster family. We found that although one member of the new family, usually the mother, might be satisfied with the placement, other members, usually siblings, might have reservations. Even so, in 15 of the 21 placements all members of the new family were very satisfied or satisfied with the placement. Using the "Rutter" adjustment scale (Rutter et al., 1972) and an independent psychologist's assessment of the children, we rated the well-being of 11 of the 21 children 18-months to two years after placement as average or above average. Thus, along with others who have assessed well-being, we found that those who came to their placements with behaviour difficulties were rarely "cured" by the two year stage. However, when the children's well-being was compared with what it had been before placement, we considered that 17 (81 per cent) had improved, and four were about the same. Overall, we rated 86 per cent of the first 22 placements (including one placement which disrupted) as successful or very successful. On the basis of whether the children were likely to have found, in Triseliotis's terms, "a family for life", we considered that 67 per cent of the placements were successful. In Chapter 4 we shall consider how these children fared five years after placement.

Rushton et al. (1988) consider the work of local authority social workers in London when they describe the first year after placement of 18 boys aged between five and nine when placed for adoption or as permanent foster children. The new parents and social workers were interviewed shortly after placement and again six and twelve months later. At the twelve month stage three had been adopted, and it was planned that another seven would be adopted. Four were permanently fostered, and there was uncertainty around the future legal status for two more. One had been returned home by the courts and one had disrupted. The children were not interviwed but the Rutter parent scales (Rutter, 1975) were used as a guide to the assessment of well-being alongside comments of social workers and parents. Thirty-one per cent were assessed as behaviourally or emotionally disturbed using this scale. The study measures outcome at too early a stage for the disruption rate to be reliable, but it offers valuable detailed information about the development of the placements in the first year, and especially about the behaviours to be found when older boys are placed with new families, and about parenting styles.

Although not specifically addressing the question of success rates, the papers on post-placement support edited by Argent (1988) focus on the importance of social work and other services as variables likely to be associated with successful outcomes.

To summarise, both large-scale surveys and qualitative studies indicate that breakdown rates for "special needs" children in care placed with new families by workers using the new methods and techniques associated with "permanence policies" are lower than for children placed in long-term foster homes by workers using more traditional methods. Success rates vary, depending on the measure of success used, and the special needs of the children, from around 95 per cent for handicapped babies, to an average of around 70 per cent for older children in care. If well-being is used as the measure of success, especially for older children, success rates tend to be lower than if success is measured in terms of breakdown rates.

THE CHILDREN WHO WERE NOT PLACED

It is easy, in looking at placements which have been made, to lose sight of those children for whom permanent placement has been deemed necessary, but who were not placed. Only the Parents for Children study and our own amongst the British studies have information about the children referred who were not placed. In America in 1982, 80,000 of the 243,000 children in foster care were freed for adoption and of these only a third were in adoptive placements. Over-represented amongst the 33,000 children waiting for an adoptive placement were minority and handicapped children, and children over the age of eleven who had been in care for four or more years. Maza (1985) further comments that, "it appears particularly difficult to find an adoptive placement for black children who are handicapped. Eighty-three per cent who are free for adoption are still waiting for an adoptive placement".

Such comprehensive details are not available for Britain, although a glance through the pages of the BAAF "Be My Parent" book, which contains details of those children whom local authorities have most difficulty in placing, would confirm that the American findings are likely to be replicated in this country. The DHSS-funded studies reported in "Social Work Decisions in Child Care" (DHSS, 1985) indicate that the majority of children coming into long-term care who are likely to be in need of permanent family placements are past infancy.

Triseliotis (1987) gives a picture of these older children who might need permanent placements, and as part of the study undertaken of adoption allowances in Scotland, Triseliotis and Hill (1986) identified 103 children in care (from 85 families) who were awaiting permanent placement. The children were most likely to be of school age, half of them being aged between eight and twelve. Over a quarter had been in care for at least six years, and 34 of the 85 families had been in care continuously for less than two years. At least one in five of those referred had had a previous experience of a permanent adoptive or foster family which had not worked out. Twenty-eight of the children still had contact with at least one parent, and 60 per cent had some contact with a member of the birth family apart from a sibling with which they were to be placed. The researchers followed-up these children ten months later when 38 per cent of the families had been placed, whilst 31 were still awaiting placement and there was a new plan for 16 which did not involve permanent family placement. Sibling groups were as likely to have been placed as those requiring placement as individuals. Half of the children aged under eleven had been placed, but only a third of those aged eleven plus. Children who were both mentally and physically handicapped were as likely to be placed as others, but children with behavioural or emotional problems were less likely to be placed.

A similar picture of those referred but not placed is reported by our own study (Thoburn et al., 1986) and by the Parents for Children researchers (National Children's Bureau, 1985) who found that only 29 per cent of the children who were aged eleven or over at referral were placed compared with 79 per cent of those who were under five, and 67 per cent of the fives to tens. Five of the nine children who were not placed in the Child Wants A Home study were aged twelve or over at the time of referral, and the majority were still in contact with members of their birth families, and uncertain about whether they were willing to allow this contact to lapse.

From this review of the evaluative literature it can be seen that those children who are most vulnerable to disruptions are also those who are least likely to be placed in the first place. We have argued elsewhere (Thoburn et al., 1987; Thoburn, 1987) that a broader definition of permanence, including different legal routes and different arrangements about contact with members of the birth family, will allow more children to find permanent new families. It would be unfortunate if the message of the research studies about the sorts of children who encounter difficulties in placement, led workers to withdraw from looking for permanent families for such youngsters.

Adoptive placements of older children and of children with problems oblige agencies to take risks. To do so implies that goals may not be reached, but not to do so also entails taking risks vis-a-vis children. Giving all children the opportunity to grow up in families they can call their own necessarily involves an element of calculated risk (Festinger, 1986).

4 Twenty-one children: five years on

We have seen from Chapter 2 that there is no consensus about measures for evaluating success. A detailed consideration of 21 children, five years after placement with new families, will now be used in order to explore the different definitions which have been found in other studies. As reported elsewhere after an earlier study of The Child Wants A Home project (Thoburn et al., 1986), these children and their new families had already been interviewed before placement, and twice up to the two-year stage. A tentative attempt at evaluating success was made, from which we concluded:

> If success is measured by the rate of placement breakdown within two years, the project can boast a 96 per cent success rate. On a combination of other criteria, the researchers rated 86 per cent of the first 22 placements as successful. This does not mean that the children had, after two years with their new families, fully recovered from the damaging effects of earlier experiences. ... At the end of the study there were still question marks over an important minority of the children placed (Thoburn et al., 1986, pp.85-86).

(Twenty-two placements are included since one broke down, and the youngster was successfully placed in a second home.)

METHODOLOGY

Small-scale qualitative studies can do no more than provide clues about factors which may be associated with success. However, they lend themselves well to an exploration of the nature of success. Although numbers are small, this is a total sample of the first 21 children placed by this experimental project, and in the first report we concluded that the children were comparable to a general population of children who are at risk of remaining long in care, and therefore possible candidates for permanent family placement. As this brief summary shows, they were indeed a "hard-to-place" group. Eleven of the children were aged ten or over at referral - thus coming into the most difficult to place category according to the larger scale survey referred to earlier (Thoburn and Rowe, 1988). Ten children were placed on their own, there were two groups of two siblings, a group of three, and a group of four. Thus there were 14 new families in all. Three were definitely placed as permanent foster children, ten were placed with the intention that the family would quickly move towards adoption, and eight were placed in permanent foster care, with the possibility of adoption left open, depending on how things went.

At the two-year stage, eight had actual contact with at least one parent at least once after placement, and in another case the adoptive mother corresponded with the birth mother. Three others had contact with siblings, and two had contact with previous foster parents - one youngster going to stay for holidays there. Only one family could be described as "exclusive" to use Holman's (1983) phrase; those others who were not in actual contact, talked readily to the youngsters about their backgrounds, and were quite willing for us to do so as researchers.

More than half of the youngsters had been abused or neglected before coming into care, and some had as many as seven "special needs" which made them "hard-to-place".

All fourteen families were asked if they would be willing to be interviewed at the five-year stage, and also if they were willing for their adopted or foster children to be interviewed. If parents agreed to this request, the older children were contacted separately. The response rate was the same as at the earlier stages, except that one family who had been interviewed previously was living abroad. This adoptive mother wrote a long letter about her adopted daughter's progress. The parents of one eight-year-old who had declined to take part in the project did so again, but wrote to say that they were perfectly satisfied with the placement and that their adopted daughter (now aged 13) was doing well. (This family had changed the Christian name as well as the surname of their child. They had since adopted another youngster and it was therefore possible to obtain the views of the social worker about the child in our sample, even though we did not interview parents, or child.) Parents who had adopted three siblings were unwilling to have the children interviewed at the first stage, and also at the five-year stage. They themselves were, however, most forthcoming and again we had access to records and discussion with the social worker who had visited during the past year.

It was not possible at this latest stage, due to the more modest nature of the study, to undertake such a thorough assessment of the youngsters as at the two-year stage. The psychologist did not visit all the children, but did go to see the two Down's children and the mentally and physically handicapped youngster as assessing their well-being and progress was considered to need her specialist skills. The Rutter parent and teacher scales (Rutter, 1975) were used at the two-year stage for those in the appropriate age range, and the parent scale was used again

40

at the five-year stage with the seven children who came into the appropriate age bracket.

Thus, 12 families were interviewed, the mother and father jointly in 10 cases, the mother alone in one case, the other being a single parent. It was possible to interview formally more of the children on this occasion since more were older. Thus, 14 children were interviewed, all on their own or as sibling groups, except for one who was interviewed together with his adoptive parents. The three who were too young or too handicapped to be formally interviewed were seen interacting with their families, as well as being assessed by the psychologist. Interviews lasted from one-and-a-half to three hours, and in two cases the parents had read the book based on our previous work, and were able to tell us where they thought we had got it right, or got it wrong.

A guided interview schedule was used, but interviews varied considerably as by this stage the key issues were different in each case. The format of the interview was similar, starting with an up-date on the previous research, and inviting comments on issues particularly relevant to the family being interviewed. They were then asked to talk about what had happened to them in the preceding three years. Parents were always seen before the children, and were asked if there were any areas of difficulty which they felt should not be brought up with the youngsters. In no case did they impose such "no go" areas, though they did suggest areas which the youngsters might find difficult or stressful.

The interviews focused on ideas about success. Parents were asked in general whether they thought the placement was successful, and were invited to talk about how they measured success. A series of specific questions was asked about different indicators of success which had been compiled from the previous study, and from the literature. Finally, they were invited to consider why the placement had been a success, a limited success, or a failure, and to discuss in particular the social work and other services offered in the preceding three years.

Two of the original social workers had left the project by this stage, and three others had joined it. The unit leader remained, and was able to comment on some of the families who had not recently been formally in touch with the agency, but who she had met in the street or at "family days". The interviews with the project social workers followed the same format as those with the families, and reports on file were also read. Some included detailed psychological assessments, or school reports.

The children ranged in age from 6 to 20, five already being over eighteen. The interview followed a similar pattern to that with the adults, though interviews tended to be shorter, and had to be fitted in around busy social schedules. Whether it was that they were more secure, further into the placement, or that by this stage they had come to know me quite well is not clear, but all the children were more forthcoming on this occasion. They gave more thought to their answers, and seemed less keen to brush me off with the first thing which came into their heads, a factor which we noted with some of them at the earlier stages.

All interviews were tape-recorded. Tapes were not transcribed, but the contents were analysed according to subject, and useful quotes

41

extracted. As on the previous occasion, anonymity for parents and children is preserved by means of slight changes in detail in the account which follows. Percentages are used despite the small numbers because this is a total sample for this agency, and because they make it easier to compare results across the different indicators. They are used descriptively and not as indicators of significant relationships.

FINDINGS

The account which follows is a summary of the evidence gathered from the different sources. It is presented in terms of nine indicators of success identified in the literature, and in the course of our inter-views with children, families, social workers and research colleagues. For each indicator, an assessment of success is made, based on the views of those principally involved, and finally a tentative assessment of overall success is offered. Where sources of information did not agree, the researcher has come down on one side or the other after considering the total picture. This somewhat stylised method of presenting findings was undertaken in order to test out the usefulness or otherwise of the different indicators of success. Inevitably, they overlap, and it is not always clear whether a particular comment is indicative, say, of "attachment" or of the youngster having found "a family for life". Many of the comments offer evidence to support more than one of these questions:

Did the placements last?

Were the children adopted?

Did the parents and children have a sense of permanence?

Did the children or young people have a sense of their own identity?

Was the children's well-being giving serious cause for concern?

Did their well-being improve?

Were the members of the new family attached to each other?

Had the youngsters found "a family for life"?

Were the children and the members of the new family satisfied with the placement?

Table 3 at the end of this chapter summarises the answers to these questions.

Did the placements last?

We have already seen that "failure", "termination", "breakdown", "disruption", and "dissolution" are all used, sometimes inter-changeably and sometimes with more specific meanings. As far as the youngsters are concerned, whether they part company with their new families before or after adoption the feelings are likely to be similar, and whatever social workers call it to soften the blow, it is likely to feel like a breakdown. Even so, it is not too easy to decide when a placement has

42

broken down given that several of the youngsters were of an age when many children leave their families. Two children had, in fact, left home in less than amicable circumstances, both at the age of 17. Another had been living away for about two months, again having left "under a cloud", but was back home temporarily when interviewed. She left again shortly afterwards when she was by then aged 18, again in angry circumstances. Thus, we can say that 19 of the 21 youngsters were still in placement at the five-year stage (including one girl who had married at the age of 18, very much with her adoptive mother's blessing).

Of the three teenagers who were living away from home, only one was assessed as definitely a "breakdown" and even here the youngster himself did not see it precisely in those terms. He still talked of his foster parents as "Mum and Dad", and used their surname. However, he had not seen them for three months at the time of our interview. He was currently living in rather seedy bed and breakfast accommodation, and explained his departure as follows:

"I thought I was getting a bit too old to stay there, and there were some young children. And part of the reason is, we didn't get on too well when I was there. We got on well at times. I think I might go up to see them on Sunday."

This placement might not have been categorised as a breakdown, if it were not for the negative comments of his former foster parents who did not envisage themselves as playing a significant role in his future life. The other two placements where the youngsters had left home were more difficult to categorise, but on balance probably should not be included in the group of those who broke down. Mary left home at 17, on New Year's Day, leaving a note to say that she could not be what her foster parents wanted her to be, and felt that she and they would be happier if she left. However, when interviewed, she described with pleasure her meetings with her "Mum" when they went for coffee and "had a laugh together". It was later learned that when her baby was born her foster mother was present at the birth. However, she was not welcome in the foster home as relationships with her foster father and especially her brothers (including a half-brother by birth), were extremely negative. The third youngster was coping well on her own and was still in touch with her adoptive family and siblings, and visiting somewhat infrequently.

Thus, depending on where one places these two, the success rate if seen in terms of non-breakdown was either 95 per cent or 86 per cent. It should be said, however, that six of the children had spent periods away from home, either regular spells of respite care, or emergency placements to allow for a "cooling-off period." One youngster was put up over-night by the project secretary, when his foster parents had reached (fortunately temporary) breaking point.

Were they adopted?

Festinger (1986) does not include in her successful placements those children who remained in their foster homes but were not adopted, and certainly some British agencies are less than pleased when families fail to proceed to adoption, even though the youngsters remain with them. By the five-year stage, 76 per cent had been adopted. Eleven were adopted within the first three years, and five in the fourth year of placement.

Thus, even those who are eventually adopted may well remain in placements as foster children for some time, a finding which has important implications for social work practice with "permanent" foster children or those fostered prior to adoption. All the children who were aged under ten at placement had been adopted, as compared with only 50 per cent of those aged ten or over. It is particularly interesting that three teenagers finally proceeded to adoption at the age of seventeen. Two of the youngsters who were not adopted until they were about to leave care were, on all the indices, amongst those most successfully placed.

In the case of five children, adoption was delayed until the local authority responsible for the youngsters had finalised its adoption allowance scheme. These included four siblings placed with the same family, and an 8-year old physically handicapped boy. In answer to the question as to what difference adoption made, Tim, who at the two-year stage had placed "wanting to be adopted" at the top of his list of three wishes, said:

"Not a lot. They treated us as if we were adopted anyway. It's just that bit of paper, that's all. But I feel a lot better for it."

His adoptive father said:

"I could have adopted him after six months. The main problem was money. He can now keep himself. He will now be a Brown properly. He definitely wants to be a Brown. The fostering or adoption - to me it didn't matter. We had less trouble with him than any of our own."

In this case a further reason for not adopting was that the time never seemed right for the adoption of his sister and, in fact, she left home without being adopted, though continuing to use the new family surname.

This raises the interesting question of whether different decisions should be made about legal status in respect of different members of sibling groups. The issue also arose with the sibling group of four, where the two youngest were placed at aged three and five, and the two eldest at 11 and 12. The eldest was not totally convinced that she wished to be placed with a new family. She was ambivalently attached to her birth mother, and told me that when the social worker had told her that she could not go back to live with her, she had just refused to believe him. In the end, she decided that she could not bear to be parted from her siblings, but joined the family after the others. Throughout the placement she agonised about whether she did or did not wish to be adopted, and whether she did or did not wish to retain contact with her birth mother. The strain of this decision was one of the reasons which pushed her into leaving home about two months before the adoption hearing was due. She returned three days before the hearing, hoping that the adoption might go ahead but this was refused because she had not been constantly in the home for the requisite period before the hearing. However, she was eventually adopted just before her 18th birthday, and then promptly left home. Her struggles with herself are documented throughout the file, and there is one very sad letter in which she and her brother beg their mother to let them be adopted. Writing this letter then caused a turbulent reaction which showed in difficult behaviour. It may have been appropriate for the youngest two

44

to have been adopted quickly, leaving the older two to come to their own decisions later, as they in fact did.

The issue of adoption or not was significant for two other youngsters, one who was adopted, and one who was not. Both placements were made with the intention of proceeding to adoption when all seemed well. Peter also at the two-year stage said that adoption was the most important of his three wishes. However, he was the youngster whose placement broke down and the "will they or won't they adopt me" issue imposed stresses throughout the placement. He strove desperately hard to fit into the family so that they would perceive him as "adoptable". However, this and no doubt the stresses of his early life led to unpredictable displays of disturbed behaviour which left the family feeling that there was no way in which he could legally be a part of their family. This youngster had been removed from his first adoptive home because of abuse, but nevertheless told us, somewhat irrationally, at the two-year stage, that the difference between fostering and adoption was that adoption was for keeps. His former foster mother said:

"Adoption didn't bring security to Peter. He had been adopted once and she kicked him out. That's just another word. He wanted the impossible. He wanted to be wanted from the start and to have what he wanted. He tried. We tried. For three years. There was no thought of him leaving. That was adopt or not adopt, but that wasn't leave us. That never entered our heads. We did spend a lot of time thinking about adopting, it might have been better if we weren't thinking about that. It would have been better if he'd been placed as a foster child, because we wouldn't have felt that awful responsibility."

Peter himself said, when interviewed outside his lodgings:

"I suppose the social workers took me away, because they [the foster parents] always said that they would never send me away. I feel as if I am adopted. The only difference is it didn't go through the court. Everybody knows me as a Jackson."

When I reminded him of his three wishes of three years ago, he said:

"If you are adopted, you feel like you belong. If you were fostered you feel just like an extra. But in my case I didn't feel like an extra."

Perhaps one of the saddest stories to which we shall return is that of Andrew. He was placed at the age of eight, had a physical disability, and had already coped with the death of his mother and rejection by his father and step-mother. He had not wanted to be placed, as this involved leaving his sisters, grandparents and aunt, and the temporary foster mother with whom he lived at weekends as he attended boarding-school. He had allowed himself to join a new family when promised that he would be allowed to stay in touch with his grandparents and sisters. At the two-year stage we rated this as a successful placement, having picked up no indication of disturbed behaviour or relationships, other than a great anxiety to do the right thing. An interim adoption order was made after two years, the full adoption order being made a year later, with an adoption allowance. When we interviewed them earlier, a 13-year old daughter of the family was strongly opposed to adoption. The foster parents were saying that they were persuaded that this was in his interest, but were determined to maintain his contact with members of his birth family even though this was difficult. His adoptive mother said:

> "The powers that be see adoption as security for a child. I can only assume they are right. I think I got cold feet just before the adoption. It should have been a warning to me. I'd got to the stage where there was no way out. Compared with other foster children we've had, I loved them - I'm not able to love Andrew."

In elaborating, she said that she felt especially guilty about not being able to love him, since she thought she ought to as she had adopted him. She also missed the support which she had welcomed when taking foster children in the past, but was unable to ask for this because Andrew was adopted and she and her husband considered that they should be fully responsible for him.

> Adoptive mother: "A child will either feel more secure by the adoption or will feel trapped. It will depend on the child." ["And you?"] - "I feel trapped. If we hadn't adopted, there would always be support. With fostering, the child does have a social worker. We have asked for relief care. But you feel so silly. That's admitting failure and that isn't an easy thing to do."

> Adoptive father: "You can say to the social worker, if the child is fostered, this child is driving me bananas, and they will perhaps explain it or give you a pat on the back. With an adopted child, you don't like to say that."

There were indications with some of the younger children that adoption was a turning point for the better for them and their parents. Macaskill (1985b), when studying some of the more problematic placements made by Parents for Children, found:

> a temporary lull in the onslaught of behavioural difficulties - as the formality of adoption receded into past history, leaving the same accumulation of problems, hope began to wane.

This did apply to one of the older placed children in our study, but a more frequently reported pattern for the younger ones was of difficult behaviour just before the adoption which the parents put down to anxiety about the hearing. Such behaviour seemed to be out of character, and abated once the order was made. It would seem that the pattern may well be different for younger children than for those placed when they are older. One family adopting three siblings aged ten, eight and seven, found that the two youngest settled in very quickly. They proceeded to adopt at around the year stage, despite pressure from the social workers to do so earlier. They felt that that was about the right length of time, but commented in terms of, the oldest:

> "It's taken a lot longer than we expected. We feel like a family now [five years after placement]. Not before. What they said was completely true about difficult behaviour. But we were expecting it after a few months."

This family did consider that it was helpful that they had already adopted, since when their oldest sister was the subject of family rows, the younger two were anxious lest this should lead to them being sent away. The parents found it helpful to be able to assure them that they were adopted and that there was no way that this would happen:

"They thought it was the start of another split up with all the rows. We'd reassure them - You're adopted - You're ours. We've got to sort things out because we've got to carry on living together. They were really frightened. It must have brought back memories for them."

Did the parents and/or children have a sense of permanence?

We have noted in Chapter 2 that American researchers (see especially Lahti, 1982) have identified a sense of permanence as being related to well-being, and not necessarily legal permanence. Considerable time during the interviews with the parents, children and social workers was spent on this issue, since it has been argued that children in foster care do not experience a sense of permanence, and that this is one of the reasons for the higher disruption rate. In our earlier report (Thoburn et al., 1986) we noted the social workers based their practice around attempts to ensure that parents and children did feel secure in the placement, and that the maximum amount of power was delegated to parents, within the limits of the boarding-out regulations. It would appear that this policy was successful since 95 per cent of the parents felt a strong sense of permanence in that they did not feel any anxiety that the youngsters would be taken away from them, unless they themselves asked for it. The one family who had some slight doubts on occasions was one where the youngster himself frequently said he wanted to leave. Whilst they accepted that this was his way of trying to hurt them, it did from time to time give them some anxieties. None of the families felt that the children would be removed by birth parents.

Foster mother: "We didn't see ourselves as foster parents for him. We thought of it as permanent from the start. We decided to play it like that. To treat him as if he were ours, even if we didn't feel he was ours. We would say, what would we do if our own son did so and so - we wouldn't have said take him away, would we?"

Thus, if the measure of a sense of permanence is taken to indicate success, 100 per cent of the parents had a strong or fairly strong sense of permanence. Fifteen of the children (71 per cent) also had a strong sense of permanence from quite early on in the placement. A further five had a sense of permanence for most of the time, which occasionally wavered. In two cases this was because younger siblings were worried that the difficult behaviour of an older brother or sister might render them vulnerable to being sent away. For three others the sense of permanence wavered because of their own uncertainty about whether they were really in the right place. The foster mother of two siblings said:

"I never thought Bill would go. I never thought Jean would stay. She told me she could not stay for ever. She'd say she was only passing through. She did try, but her trying was a different way to us, but that was her personality. That couldn't be helped. It's hard to believe, when people come round here, I don't think they think for one minute that he's any different - that he's adopted - and, of course, he isn't any different. He just isn't."

When I asked Jean if she had ever felt worried that she would be taken away, she said:

> "At one time I hoped they would. I hated it so much there. She thought I was a bit cuckoo at one time and she sent me down to the hospital. I knew I couldn't be what she wanted. I just wanted to go out and do what I wanted to do. I used to run away all the time. Just to get out of the house. I couldn't handle it. I wanted to be what they wanted me to be at that time. But I just couldn't manage it."

Interestingly, when her foster mother arranged for the social worker to come so that Jean could tell her this, she said nothing. None of the children actually said during the research interviews that they felt they might be sent away, but it was clear from the descriptions of his behaviour that the youngster who did eventually leave, was constantly afraid that he would be taken or sent away. This emerged consistently through all our interviews during the course of the placement. Consequently he was terrified of reviews, and of visits from the local authority social worker, since he knew that his behaviour would be under review. He was the only one who was considered to have a poor sense of permanence.

If one includes those with a strong sense of permanence (71 per cent, and those with a fairly strong sense of permanence but some slight uncertainty (23 per cent), we find that 95 per cent of the children could be seen as successful or fairly successful on this measure. In discussing this, and the advantages and disadvantages of fostering and adoption, the youngsters frequently brought up the subject of names. Only the three permanently fostered children, who moved to their new homes in their teens and had contact with members of their birth families, did not take on the surname of the new family. Several parents and children mentioned their irritation when doctors, dentists, or previous social workers, refused to use the new name. Several recounted instances of sitting in the doctor's waiting-room refusing to move when the wrong name was called. Once the youngsters left school things became even more complicated, with parents being unsure as to what name to use for work and insurance card purposes, and bank accounts. One foster mother was told she could not open a Post Office account in the new name. She therefore went to another Post Office and didn't ask their permission to do so. It was when he realised that he would have to use his birth name when he got married that one youngster finally decided he must be adopted before he was 18, although he also said that had this not been possible, he would just have changed his name by Deed Poll.

Early in the placement several of the children commented that social work practice did lead to a sense of insecurity. Several were made anxious by reviews. Later on they were less bothered by this and seemed to enjoy social work visits more. However, the older children commented on the embarrassment they experienced when workers had to check up on friends if they wished to stay the night. Mary commented:

> "I wanted to be adopted. Because David [the social worker] or someone would say, 'You're in the care of Social Services' and it used to make me really angry. You didn't know who you were supposed to be. I didn't ever feel they'd take me away though."

When I asked Tim if he had any tips for social workers he said:

"Reviews. I hated them. I'm glad I don't have to have any more. The worst thing about care was having a social worker come to see you. Who ever it was. It didn't matter who it was. You didn't feel as if you were a normal child because you had a social worker coming to see you. Tips to pass on? I can't because I am not a social worker myself. I'm glad I'm not a social worker because I'd be disliked by a lot of people. Because they are generally disliked."

Did the children and young people have a sense of their own identity?

Several research studies (see especially Weinstein, 1960, Thorpe, 1980; and Fanshel and Shinn, 1978) have identified a link between well-being and a sense of identity. Studies of adult adoptees have singled out confusion about identity as a significant problem for some adopted people, especially those who decide to search out their birth parents. (See especially Triseliotis, 1973). Indeed, The Children's Society project which is the subject of this chapter has recently conducted a series of seminars on the theme of adoption and identity for members of the "adoption triangle".

The concept of identity is complex, and several questions were asked around this area to try to get a picture of how the youngsters saw themselves, and particularly whether they had integrated their past and present identities, and valued themselves, and were valued for the people they had become.

Triseliotis, in an important article on this subject (1983, pp.22-23) notes that, "concepts such as identity, security, sense of belonging are elusive and difficult to define or measure." He believes, however, that despite these difficulties an attempt to do so must be made by those researching adoption and fostering, and offers the following definition:

"Personal identity is the result of multiple psychological, social and cultural influences which combine towards the building of an integrated and unified self. By personal identity I mean the kind of consciousness we all carry about - who we are and the kind of self-image we have of ourselves. Depending on its quality and strength, the sense of self gives us a feeling of separateness from others, distinguishing us from our environment, whilst at the same time enabling us to enter into daily social interactions and relationships with a degree of confidence."

He identifies three areas which make a contribution to identity building:

"1) a childhood experience of feeling wanted and loved within a secure environment;

2) knowledge about one's background and personal history; and

3) the experience of being perceived by others as a worthwhile person."

It has already been noted that two years after placement, ten youngsters had contact with either birth parents or siblings. At the five-year stage, one child was still in touch with both parents, and

49

three still had good contact with their mothers. Four others, though not in actual contact, were aware of the life circumstances of their parents because they were in touch with siblings who were, in turn, in contact with a parent. Four were still in regular contact with siblings. The adoptive mother of a six-year old Down's child corresponded about once a year with her birth mother, and was able to feed comments about her to the youngster and help her to understand about having had another Mummy. (This was made easier by the placement of a second Down's youngster whose birth mother visited the new family.) Another adopted boy of 13 still occasionally went to stay with a family who had played an important "aunt and uncle" role for him whilst he had been in residential care. This was the only example of a child still in contact with previous carers, although the adoptive parents of a young physically and mentally handicapped boy still wrote to his previous foster parents.

One would have expected these children to have a reasonably good sense of their past, even if no longer in contact with people from the past, since they had been well-prepared for placement, and had almost all worked on life story books. Several of them brought out these books when we talked, in order to help me to understand what they were saying about their past. None of the parents or children interviewed showed any reluctance to discuss birth families, and all the new parents conveyed positive feelings about the birth families. It was known from the file, and discussion with the social worker who had recently visited whilst placing a second child, that the one set of parents not interviewed were reluctant to allow the youngster to talk freely about her birth family.

Thus, 76 per cent of the children had had some contact with important people from the past after their placement, and 57 per cent still had contact at the five-year stage. With about half of the families where there was still actual contact, it was the new parents who made the biggest effort to keep things going. The foster mother of the 17-year old lad who was about to be adopted, told how she had helped him to write letters to his sisters, as he did not find it easy to write. The sisters who had remained in their Children's Home until becoming independent seem to have negotiated adult life quite well. They lived some distance away but were going to come to the adoption/18th birthday party. She said - "I wanted him to keep in touch because I think that's right. If it was me - I'd see them more." The lad confirmed that he was always pleased to hear from them and was looking forward to seeing them again.

In other cases the social workers and the youngsters took the initiative in keeping up contact. In the early stages of placement parents used to visit the new families' homes. By the five-year stage, contact tended to be in the project office, or at the home of the birth parents. This arrangement was felt to be more appropriate by the youngsters, now in their late teens, and by the adoptive or foster families.

All those older children who were no longer in touch with birth parents were asked if they would be likely to look them up when they were old enough, and some were of an age to have done so already. Only one youngster had made tentative moves towards finding his birth family. This was the lad who had had a previous failed adoption, and was drifting somewhat rootlessly. The stresses of coping with life had overwhelmed him so that he had temporarily given up his search, but said he would probably try again later when he felt more settled. The 18-year old who was about to have her own baby said of her mother:

> "I don't want to know anything about her. I feel really angry when I talk about her. I wouldn't mind meeting my real Dad if I could find him."

A handicapped youngster, placed at 8 and now 13, and well-settled with his adoptive family, said in front of his adoptive Mum and Dad:

> "Just lately - I don't know why it is - I keep having dreams. I wonder what my Mum's doing now. How my Dad's doing, what my sisters are doing. My Mum has blonde hair and is tall. My Dad is like me. I just think - Oh, how it would have been nice if they liked me more. I could have seen them. I would have liked to have done. If they'd given me a bit more of a chance than I had. In my dreams, sometimes I feel a bit sad for my Mum and Dad, because if they had given me more time, I thought, I could have planned my future. I see pictures in my dreams of what I'd have liked to have done with my sisters."

His adoptive mother responded by telling him about the possibilities of looking up his family when he was 18, and thought that his sisters might come to stay with him some time. This youngster had been abused and neglected, and had returned home and been abused again. He was totally committed to finding a new family, and was the one whose first placement had disrupted after three months.

Another lad, not in touch with birth parents but in touch with siblings, had found the life story work extremely difficult as he had wanted to see himself as part of his new family so firmly from the start, and hated any discussion of his earlier life. On completing his life story work he had come back home, gone upstairs, and torn the book in half, bringing it downstairs to his foster mother and saying, "That's what I think of it, a waste of your time and a waste of my time." However, six months or so before we interviewed him, he was much more at peace with himself and his past. He had been chatting to the mother of one of his friends about life in the Children's Home, and had told her about his book, and taken it to her. She had rewritten the story for him in a new book. He said that he was now very glad to have it as it was useful to be able to make sense of the past. He did not think he would look up his birth parents but was glad to be in touch with his sisters.

All those who were still in touch with members of their birth families were pleased about this. In response to a comment from the interviewer that some people said that it was confusing to children to have two families, a 14-year old replied very promptly, "I don't find it confusing, because I know what's what. I like going to see Grandad. He's a laugh." When asked if he would have come to this family if it had not been possible for him to stay in touch with his birth relatives, he said, again very firmly, "No, I wouldn't." However, his adoptive parents were finding it very difficult to attach to him and were not sure whether the contact should have been started in the first place. When I asked if they would like to terminate it now, the adoptive mother said:

"I don't see how that would benefit us. I wish I'd never set eyes on
any of them - but severing contact - I can't see the point. I see
no way forward - because obviously he'd like to live with his family
- like any foster child. H'd like to go to live with his sister.
With hindsight - it should have been cut off. We wouldn't recommend
adoption with contact. It's cruel to the kid. I don't think there
is an easy answer. There isn't a cure. The whole thing is so
messy."

Whether they had contact or not, most children primarily identified with
their new families, with five still identifying to some extent with
their birth families also. Six were still confused to greater or lesser
extents about how their past fitted in with their present. The adoptive
mother of a 17-year old said:

"Maggie [natural parent] is her real Mum. You still get the feeling
"that's my real Mum, my real family". Not with the others, but with
Angie. Sometimes she uses her other surname and sometimes ours."

Following Triseliotis' definition, we considered not only whether the
children had successfully integrated their past with their present but
also, in assessing their sense of identity, whether they felt valued as
people in their own right. The principal source of evidence had to be
the children themselves, although the way in which their new parents
talked about them also helped to build up a picture. Thus, when a
foster father talked with great pride of his 17-year old son, to the
extent that his eyes watered with emotion, it seemed not unreasonable to
assume that this obvious affection would have communicated itself to the
youngster and contributed to his sense of being a "worthwhile person".
His sister, who had left the home, had not felt valued for the person
she was. In the note she wrote when she was leaving, she said:

"I've gone to live with my friend. I'm not telling you where it is.
I think if you'd got another girl it would have been alright. I'm
sorry I'm not the girl you wanted me to be."

When interviewed she said:

"That didn't really work from the start. Everything I did was wrong
in Mum's eyes. I wanted to be what they wanted me to be at that
time. But I knew I never could be."

Some youngsters were still trying to cope with the confusion they felt
about not being a "worthwhile person" in the eyes of their birth
parents:

Adoptive mother of 10-year old: "To a certain extent she is still
confused. I think the most difficult thing - the thing she still
can't understand - 'why can my mother look after the two girls who
are still with her when she couldn't look after me?' She doesn't
talk about it, but I'm sure she feels it. There was absolutely no
way she would meet her mother when she came for the adoption
hearing."

Adoptive mother of siblings: "I won't mind them contacting her. I
say - it's still your mum and dad when all is said and done.
Actually I do feel they felt like they'd been deserted. I've tried
to get across to them that she was thinking of the best for them.

Fred felt very bitter about that - her consenting to the adoption. He thinks he is a social outcast because he is adopted. A lot of the rowing - it's about trying to split us up. I've said, 'Row as much as you like. You won't split us up.' He didn't."

An adoptive father told how, four years after placement, after a long spell of very difficult behaviour, their adopted teenage son spoke for the first time of an incident when his father was physically abusing his mother. She had told him to get help, and he had done nothing, being fond of both parents and not knowing whose side to take. He said he blamed himself for the break-up of the marriage and for his and his sisters' going into care. Even the reassurance of being adopted did not help him to feel good about himself.

On the other hand, another lad showed clearly that he had come to value himself as a person by saying that he thought he was now doing so well his parents would regret not having kept him with them if they knew of his progress.

A sense of racial identity should also be considered for the two black youngsters. Neither had a particularly strong sense of pride in their race, and both identified very strongly with their new families. However, both were willing to talk to us about being black in a white family in an area where there were very few black people. The 10-year old thought about our questions, and answered carefully, but seemed bored by them and somewhat perplexed that we thought the issue important. He had encountered some racism, but said he did not let it bother him. His parents, who had had to cope with the results of a car accident in which the mother had been seriously injured, felt that they had not done enough to help him develop a positive sense of his identity as a black person, but were thinking of ways of doing so.

A mixed parentage teenager, referring to remarks about his colour, said:

"They all say it as a joke, and I take it as a joke. I used to get upset that they did it. That's why my dad did it all the while. But I got used to it. Now when my mates do it, it doesn't bother me."

When asked if he would have liked to have been placed with a mixed parentage family, he said:

"I don't think it would have bothered me if they were as good as the ones I've got now."

Using Triseliotis's definition as a guideline for our assessment, it was concluded that six of the children had a good sense of identity, and a further 10 had a fairly good sense of identity, but with some confusion or uncertainty. (Seventy-six per cent of the total were in either of these two categories). There were serious doubts about the sense of identity of three of the youngsters; one we assessed as having a poor sense of identity, and one youngster was so mentally and physically handicapped that the concept seemed not applicable.

<u>Was the "well-being" of the youngster rated a cause for concern?</u>

It was noted in Chapter 2 that several researchers have attempted to assess well-being and that this, like identity, is an elusive concept. The well-being of children who had a disability was compared with that of other children in the general population with the same mental or physical handicap. (It would be unreasonable to compare the well-being of a youngster with a mental handicap with a youngster of the same age who did not have that mental handicap.) When considering the well-being of the other youngsters, the frame of reference was that of children of similar ages living in similar material circumstances to those in which the youngsters would have been living had they not come into care. Lack of a control group must make this assessment tentative. The rating of well-being was based on what the parents, youngsters, and social workers said about the children's lives, and about any problems they were experiencing. These accounts were supplemented by records which mostly included school reports, accounts of delinquent episodes and court appearances, or abuse of drugs or alcohol. Patterns of employment were an indicator of well-being for the older children, and for all children questions were asked about their ability to make and keep friends. For seven children between the ages of 8 and 15, who were not mentally handicapped, the Rutter parent scale was used (Rutter et al., 1975).

As observed in Chapter 2, especially in considering Macaskill's work (1985b), placement with a new family, and even the commitment of adoption, cannot be expected to cure disturbed behaviour, at least in the short-term. Triseliotis and Russell (1984) found that 36 per cent of youngsters caused concern at some stage during their childhood because of their behaviour or emotional problems, but conclude on the more hopeful note that most youngsters grew through these difficulties as they moved into adult life. Discussions with the parents in this study, and indeed the children themselves, supported these findings, in that the majority of youngsters placed beyond infancy did cause concern to their new parents. Leaving aside the three handicapped youngsters, whose parents described behaviour which was quite difficult to handle, but which they attributed to the handicap rather than to individual disturbance, (for example, being extremely lively in the early hours of the morning, or constantly repeating things "parrot-fashion"), the parents of only three youngsters said that they had had no concerns about behavioural or emotional difficulties at any stage in the placement.

At the referral and two-year stages behavioural disturbance and emotional disturbance were considered separately, and a similar distinction could be made from parents' and social workers' comments at the five-year stage. Ten of the children had had behaviour problems at some time in the past, and in three cases these were serious. At the time of the last interview, five had behaviour problems - in one case of a serious nature, thus indicating some improvement in this respect. Nine had emotional problems earlier in the placement, and in three cases these were serious problems. At the five-year stage eight had emotional problems, and in three cases these were serious problems. There was confirmation for Fahlberg's thesis (1981) that whilst behavioural disturbance, (as evidenced by acting out behaviour, or temper tantrums), may help attachment, emotional disturbance is much more difficult for parents to cope with, and more likely to lead to break down. At the two-year stage we noted, "the marked discrepancy in at least two cases between behaviour at home (reported as good) and behaviour at school (poor)" (Thoburn et al., 1987, p.82). In one case we had assessed that the placement was likely to break down, whereas three years later the youngster was firmly attached to his family, had just been adopted, was well-settled in a permanent job, and he and his parents could joke about the times when they had nearly, or actually, thrown him out.

> Philip: "They wouldn't kick me out, you would't kick me out, would you Mum?"

> Mum (laughing): "Well, not permanently, anyway."

When children were acting out their frustrations, schools seemed to have more difficulty coping than did their parents. Parents described this behaviour in similar terms - the youngster going through quite prolonged periods of "winding them up" and eventually provoking a scene, sometimes with violence or threatened violence on the part of the youngster, or physical punishment on the part of the parents.

> Foster mother: "He had one smack - a few months after he came. He wanted it. That seemed as if he wanted it. He wanted to see how far he could go. He put his fist up. I said, right. I put him over my knee and smacked his backside as hard as I could. He went upstairs and he did cry and came down and apologised and I said 'That's alright, Bill, but you know now.' And he never ever looked back. That did something to him. He seemed to want it."

> Adoptive mother: "Once I was really frightened of Andy. Sitting here now, thinking about it, I was more worried than I need have been. He's fine now. Normally his tempers came out of the frustration of school."

On that occasion the parents had phoned the social worker after about two days of constant provocation, and insisted that Andy be taken away for 24-hours to give him a chance to think through whether he really wanted to be with them. By that stage he was 15, and had been with his new family for almost four years:

> "He'd been so bad. Played truant. Wouldn't go to school. We searched his room for drugs. Mark [husband] had to take the day off work. We told the social worker, either he got him to agree he'd obey the rules or find somewhere else to live. It paid off. He came back 24-hours later. He didn't need to say anything. After that I knew everything was going to be alright. I never really had any doubts about him coming back. If I had had, I wouldn't have done it. He never wanted to talk about the past but he'd obviously been thinking about it. He didn't want us to know he'd been thinking about it. This was the way it had been coming out."

Another parent described her 14-year old adopted son as follows:

> "We knew he was a bit volatile. He had a lot of arguments with the house-mother. His tempers were very sudden. He showed it in the first few months, and then it got better. He'd fly off the handle, but it would be over in a few minutes. He had to win and he had to

be in everything. He got close to us, and then he drifted away. He was suspended for being abusive to the teachers. He kept winding me up. From anything a row would start. What time will dinner be - 7 o'clock - because it was a minute past, he wanted a row about it."

In another case, where a youngster was both emotionally and behaviourally disturbed, the parents were almost relieved when there was an incident which allowed tensions to be released:

> Foster mother: "After about three years, I was smacking him like he was three - he was 15 - smacking his bottom. It hurt my hand more than his bottom. He liked it. It made him feel I was his Mum and that mattered."

After one severe piece of provocation, which mother, father and youngster agreed merited "a good hiding", his foster father hit him across the mouth. This was dealt with as an abuse incident, and the parents felt that the way it had been handled by the social workers had led to a lessening of their willingness to go on trying.

Emotional difficulties, which at the two-year stage were described as "symptoms such as nervous habits or mannerisms, eating problems, withdrawn behaviour, eneurisis, psychosomatic symptoms, lying constantly and unnecessarily, or excessively anxious or obsessional behaviour" (Thoburn et al., 1986) were much more difficult to cope with throughout the placement. When such youngsters were told off, instead of shouting back or putting up their fists, they would slam the door and go into their room for hours on end. Behaviour was characterised by long silences, or attempts to please which didn't quite come off:

> Adoptive father: "David (aged 14) hadn't spoken to us for days. We started to push him, to provoke him. There's nothing there. The box is empty. He's in one corner and we're in the other, and there's nothing in between to fill it. He cries easily. He looks in a trance. He will sit for hours. He can't be happy with us. If he throws things, or has a temper tantrum, you've got something to work with, but there's not a spark."

> Adoptive father of a 10-year old: "He goes along in a dream world a lot of the time and doesn't concentrate on what he is doing. He is a passive sort of person. He is easy because of that. But that can be quite a debit. It looks wonderful to people outside, but it can be irritating. It would be easier if he was less accommodating. I know part of what has happened between us is about me almost goading him to try to get him actually to show me who and what he actually is and is feeling."

> Adoptive mother about a 10-year old: "She is afraid of change, she's very young for her age. She doesn't want to grow up. She doesn't have a temper like the others, but she gets back at you. You tell her off, but she won't say anything. She'll draw on her clothes with felt-tips. She'll get shoe-polish all down her dress. That's the way she gets back at me. Her temper is internalised, it makes her clumsy. She is insolent at school. That's what you get. If she doesn't want to do anything, she won't."

The two pieces of behaviour which parents found most difficult to cope with, were lying, and "making use of us":

"He still rarely tells the truth.   He'd do anything rather than tell the truth."

"The most difficult thing?   Constant lying - about anything and everything.   Their first answer is almost always a lie.   It's ever so silly,   and when they have done something,   to try to get to   the bottom of   it - it can take for ever.   They can tell you   one   lie after another and they can sound so convincing.   They're so good at it.   You feel - can't they trust me after all this time?"

"Adam doesn't want to be part of our family.   He wants to use someone. He thinks that is what people are for.   All children do to some extent, mind you.   If things were nice for him, he'd turn round and kick you in the teeth.   Always when things were at their   best. He didn't know what love was.   It worries me.   He'll meet a girl and get married.   I dread what his reaction to children will be."

Whilst   there   was a tendency for behaviourally disturbed children   to get gradually better, with explosive episodes becoming less frequent, or - a   more   common   pattern - petering out after   some   major   crisis   or turning-point,   the   emotionally disturbed children,   despite periods of trying   very hard,   either made very slow progress or got   progressively worse.

Foster father of child placed when aged 12:   "I've got to say,   her time   here wasn't very nice for us - or for her.   There were   times when she was up,   and we'd think to ourselves, we've done it - she's lovely. She would always think about you, birthdays and that, she'd get her   little bit in,   but every time   anything   like   that   was happening,   she was pulling one over on us.   You can't do a lot with a   liar.   Why do   they go and say rubbish like   that?   - the   most ridiculous things you've ever heard.   What our social worker told us about them all came up.   I thought we've now brought up three of our own - there's no way a little 'un would get one round me.   But   she was   right.   You think they are exaggerating - the social   workers. Perhaps she was too old when she came."

As   far   as schooling was concerned,   eight were of above   average   or average   ability,   six   were of below average ability,   and   seven   were educationally   handicapped.   The   behaviour   at school of four   of   the children was above average,   for seven it was average,   and for nine   it was   below average or   poor,   with four having been excluded from school at   some   stage.   One child was being educated at home as a   result   of parental choice.

Using   conflict with the law or other deviant behaviour as   indicators of well-being,   eight of the children had been involved in some form   of delinquency, mostly stealing, but only one youngster had appeared before the court.   At the time of interview she had already three convictions for   assault,   and   one drugs offence recorded against her   and   was   to appear at court for breaching a probation order.   Two had been involved with   drugs,   and   two   were   said to   drink   quite   heavily.   Six   had difficulty making or keeping friends, and in three cases this difficulty was serious.

Ten youngsters were of working age. Three of these were at adult training centres, but five of the other seven had got jobs straight from school and were showing every sign of having a good work record. All these were in manual occupations and the foster or adoptive parents had taken a major part in helping the youngsters to get jobs. The other two had done quite well on YTS schemes, but once these had finished, they had been drifting from one casual job to the next, or were unemployed. Both of these had serious debt problems, and were living in precarious housing situations.

To end this section on well-being, it should be said that three of the youngsters who were mentally handicapped and placed as babies were rated as of above average well-being, and had shown no behaviour problems other than those to be expected in youngsters with their particular handicap. The lad, whose first placement had broken down and who was at the time described as being very disturbed indeed, had settled extremely well in his new family and was no longer rated as disturbed. Two other youngsters, described as disturbed and of low academic ability when placed as teenagers from their Children's Homes, had settled with almost no problems:

> Adoptive mother of a 20-year old who is now married: "I don't think we have had any real problems with Amy during the adjustment to adult life. She has always been very close to me, once she had settled within the family. She would talk to me and ask my advice on any subject. She enjoyed her life here once she started work. She was a very hard-working girl, well-liked by her workmates. She is a very kind hearted girl and extremely generous. She writes to me regularly and tells me how much she likes married life. She had got their flat very homely and comfortable by the time we left the area, a month after her marriage. She is still inclined to be a bit scatterbrained, and lots of the time only half listens to some things, and this sometimes causes problems for her. However, as far as we are concerned, she has grown up into a nice young woman, a far cry from the Amy that came to me, and I have no regret whatsoever about adopting her."

Taking into consideration these various indicators of well-being, 67 per cent were rated as of average well-being or above, and 33 per cent as of below average or poor well-being.

Did the children's well-being improve after placement?

Given the difficulties which many of the children had experienced before placement, it should come as no surprise that five years in a loving and consistent home had nevertheless not been enough to make the resultant problems disappear. A more appropriate measure, therefore, might be whether the youngsters had improved. At the two-year stage 52 per cent of the children had been rated as being of at least average well-being, so that with 67 per cent being given this rating at the five-year stage, there was some measure of improvement in the next three years. However, these ratings do not apply necessarily to the same children, with five children being rated more highly at the five-year stage, and two youngsters who were rated as average being assessed as below average or poor. There were Rutter scales for five children at both the two-year and five-year stages. In four cases, children who were rated as showing some disturbance at the two-year stage did not do so five years after placement, whilst one youngster who on this scale appeared not to come into the "disorder" category, (rating: 6), was showing serious signs of disturbance at the five-year stage (rating: 30).

Thirteen children (62 per cent) were considered to be much improved or improved since placement, whilst eight were considered to be the same. Only one of the children was rated as of lower well-being than at the time of placement.

Were the members of the new family attached to each other?

"Attachment" is often discussed as if it were a simple concept. In fact, it is extremely complex. (See Bowlby (1979) for a discussion of the concept of "attachment", and the making of "affectional bonds". The term "attachment" is used here to mean a close, loving, and lasting relationship, rather than in the precise sense of psychological literature.) Attachment must be considered between each member of the family, and in either direction. Thus, a youngster may be attached to the mother but the mother not to him or her. The same youngster may or may not be attached to other members of the family. Evidence about attachment was drawn from interviews, and also from observing the youngsters with members of their families. In general terms, it was more likely that new parents would be attached to children, than the children to them. It was least likely that the natural children of the new family would be attached to the youngster placed with them, and vice versa. Mothers were more likely to be attached to the youngsters than fathers. In one case, the marriage had broken, the youngster subsequently being adopted by the foster mother, who later re-married. There was one single parent, a divorcee. She had adopted three Down's youngsters, the one in our study being of very high ability for someone with this condition. Her mother told us with some humour that Janet had taken it upon herself to look for a Daddy, and was liable to invite any suitable males she came across to take on this role.

In 12 cases youngsters were attached to all members of the family, and all family members to them. The mother who had asked for her aggressive and threatening teenage foster child to be removed over night for a "cooling off period" was one of these; she never really had doubts about his coming back, because she was quite sure that a mutual attachment existed. Several of the older youngsters, at times of anger or frustration, dared their parents to send them back. Those who were attached were not threatened by this.

> Foster father: "I never felt threatened by his saying that he wanted to go back where he came from."

Some parents at previous interviews had talked about falling in love with their youngster very quickly. For others it took more time.

> Mother of a 10-year old: "You don't expect it to be instantaneous. It's a slow process. You gradually, over five years, grow together

more and more. There is no question of falling in love instantaneously. We're happier as a family now, more integrated. I couldn't imagine him not being there. I never questioned that Philip was <u>mine</u>. One has to make a distinction between the sense of his being yours, and attachment."

Other parents greatly regretted that when their five-year old had joined them, they had not been guided by their instincts and kept the youngster away from school until she had felt closer:

Mother: "Sometimes I think Mary could have done with more individual attention. I think the biggest mistake with her - we should have insisted on her staying at home for a while. I can actually remember thinking I wished she'd be ill. She was so independent. I <u>could</u> have babied her."

In the case where the family did withdraw a child of a similar age from school, they were convinced that this had facilitated the attachment process.

Some parents gave evidence of attachment to youngsters, whom they felt were not attached to them:

Foster mother: "I didn't see it as a job the first year or so. I have recently. It is something to do with, you say to yourself, you are doing a good job. But there is another thing which I can't explain. How difficult it is, even on a bad day, just to say goodbye. They are part of you in one sense. I worry about them. I find I react exactly every way like I do with my own children. <u>We</u> feel they are part of our family. It's just the other way <u>round</u>. You don't get the affection. At their age, you don't expect a lot of it. You don't expect to see the best of any youngster if they come to you at 12 or 13."

In some cases parents gave us mixed messages about their attachment to the youngsters, usually those who had left home in somewhat fraught circumstances. Whereas a critical incident in some cases had improved attachment, in others it had closed the doors. As we shall see in Chapter 5 the parents viewed the way the social workers handled such situations as being crucial in determining which way things would go. One family said, "We coped for a long time. There was light at the end of the tunnel." They then described how a mishandled incident had made them feel the effort was not worth it. Even after their youngster had left, however, they felt some affection for him, and would have left doors open if the social worker had taken on the role of conciliator. The sadness in this case was that the youngster also would have liked this to have happened, but lacked the skills to open the doors for himself. There was in this case remarkable congruence between what the youngster told us and what his former foster parents told us. When asked directly if they still felt affection for him, the mother said, "That's difficult. We're not even honest with ourselves. I <u>vow</u> I won't let him come in. But if he was standing there on the doorstep ... ?"

A teenager said, "I sometimes wonder whether they really love me." Her adoptive mother said:

"She does very well provided all goes well - but the least little thing becomes like a mountain. She's inconsiderate. She gets told off and gets resentful. She does say sorry, but she might as well be saying 'hard cheese'. When she went, I thought it had all been just surface. She started talking about 'my real mother'. But before she went away, we were like sisters. She was too old to have a proper mother, but we got on very well."

An important point is illustrated here. Even when attachments develop between parents and older children, they are often not conventional parent-child attachments. One of the social workers considered that this was one reason why some of the youngsters placed in their mid-teens were more successful than those placed in their early teens. It was seen as helpful that there could be no pretence of a full mother-daughter relationship. She described one adoptive mother as:

"a sort of Aunty. A very successful Aunty. It was like a relation-ship with a good step-mother or a good aunt. This was acknowledged. She took on a 15-year old. She was good at parenting in a different way."

Both parents were considered to be attached or fairly well attached in 15 cases, and the mother only to be attached in three cases (including the single parent). Thus, in 81 per cent of cases a parent was attached or fairly well attached to the youngster. In two cases parents were ambivalently attached and in one case neither parent was attached. Where there were natural children of the family (12 cases), they were well or fairly well attached in seven cases, but definitely not in five cases. In one family, where - against all research and practice wisdom - parents with a three-year old had taken a child of five in part as a companion to that youngster, there was a very strong bond between these two children, which was perhaps stronger than that between the youngster and his adoptive parents. It is worth noting that this family worked hard to form attachments, and had deliberately kept both children out of school, and allowed the five-year old to regress. The parents thought that the three-year old had made this more possible by allowing him to share her bottle.

As already noted, children were less likely to be attached to parents. Whilst all those asked directly if they felt they really loved their new parents said they did, it was obvious from other parts of the interviews and especially from reported behaviour, that some of them were not describing a deep attachment or were ambivalently attached. Twelve children were attached to all members of the family, and two to the mother only. Five were ambivalently attached, and two were not attached. With some of these ambivalently attached youngsters there was some hope still that they would become more fully attached. It seemed possible, for instance, that now that she was away from the home, with a consequent reduction of stress on the whole family, one youngster would be able to consolidate the attachment she and her foster mother felt for each other. Some youngsters gave us very mixed messages. One teenage mentally handicapped lad, when asked about the most important person in his life, mentioned his natural step-brother whom he had not seen for about four years. However, he always insisted on his foster mother tucking him up in bed, and giving him a cuddle and reading a bedtime story. One 14-year old who was physically handicapped passed on the following tips to other youngsters in a similar position. He was, indeed, in a good position to do so having made three previously failed attempts at permanent family placement:

> "You give your Mum and Dad time to adapt to you - and don't think you are going to order them about. I went over the top a bit when I was at the Briggs's. You've got to pull your weight. There is no way you will get the whole family after you. Don't expect too much of them. They won't expect too much of you. If anyone is going to get along, they've got to be able to talk about things - the past and the future, whatever it is. I think you'd want to talk about it once you knew the people you were with."

Had the youngsters found "a family for life"?

A study of the literature about why permanence policies have been developed leads to the conclusion that finding a family for life could be viewed as the most important indicator of success. If so, the project studied must indeed be rated as highly successful, since it was estimated that 19 (90 per cent) had indeed found "a family for life". Seven children were in the happy position of having two families in that they still had good contact with their birth families.

Five families were rated positively, even though the relationship was not likely to be too close. Included here were mentally handicapped youngsters who would be likely to be in some form of sheltered accommodation or hostel, but would be remaining in touch with their extended foster or adoptive families. Similarly included were older members of sibling groups who, whilst not very well attached to the parents, would remain in firm contact with their younger siblings who had become fully integrated with their new families.

Of the two who had probably not found a family for life, one did at least have good contacts with his birth family, so that only one youngster was in the unhappy position of having no caring adult who would be available to provide support at times of difficulty in his future life. The birth mother of one teenager, although originally intending to contest the adoption, had given her consent verbally at the hearing, and said to the adoptive mother about her daughter who had been away and returned, "I'm ever so pleased Pat's come back to you." The sister, who was firmly attached to the new family, said, about her birth mother, "She's doing alright for herself now. I don't feel much for her now. But I know Pat does a lot - still."

In describing how fully integrated into the family a youngster placed at eleven had become, one father said:

> "They're all the same [his four sons, including the adopted youngster] - they all go out together like a family. I would say it's flawless. We could have had ten like him. I think in his own head, he thinks we're his Mum and Dad, and this is his family."

The mother of a youngster who had left home, on the other hand, exemplifies one of those cases where there was probably a lifetime relationship between mother and daughter, but it would not be allowed to get too close on either side:

"To tell you the truth, I was glad when she left home. I said if
that's what you want, that's what I want. I'd had enough. I'd
never have told her to go. But I was relieved. Everyone else told
her she'd have to go. But I would come back through the gate and
she'd be trotting behind me and they'd be furious. She couldn't
have been happy here. That was sad to see her. At one point we
were getting really close, and you'd think it's worth it. You'd try
again - you'd think she's a really good kid, really, and then -
BANG. I can't say there's a lot there now. But I'd like to see her
settled. When we see each other, I enjoy it - I love it. We have a
laugh together."

The youngster said:

"Mum nagged me. I hated the boys. That didn't really work from the
start. Everything I did was wrong in Mum's eyes. But she says
she'll never give up trying with me. I'm the sort of person who
won't be told what to do by anyone. Both of them have told me they
love me. I know she's there if I ever need anything. She told me
that. I'm a lot happier now because I am doing what I want to do.
I wish we'd got on like we do now when I was living at home."

In those cases where older siblings felt less a part of the new
family than the others they tended to feel some sadness that they were
unable to share their mixed feelings with their brothers and sisters
because the younger ones were reluctant to talk about the past. Also,
there was usually a mismatch of affection, with the older child being
more attached to the younger ones, than the other way round. It was as
if the younger siblings, having thrown in their lot with the new family,
were not willing to have their equilibrium disturbed by the lasting
sadness of the older child. Thus, one teenager, when starting the
interview, immediately asked if we had seen her brother, whereas the
brother told us that he was not interested in talking about his sister
and wasn't bothered if he saw her or not.

The three children placed as handicapped babies made an interesting
group. One had turned out to be far more mentally handicapped than his
new family had anticipated and indeed they had specifically said that
they could cope with a physical handicap, but not with a mental
handicap. However, he was clearly very much loved by both parents and by
the extended family who would go on caring for him even if something
unfortunate happened to his adoptive parents. The two Down's children
were by the five-year stage both living in households with other Down's
children. One had been adopted by a family who already had a Down's
youngster, and the other had since adopted two more Downs's youngsters.
Both these parents said how well the youngsters got on together and that
their hope for the future was that they would be able to move into
independent but supervised living together.

It seemed likely that seven of the youngsters would never be able to
live fully independently because of their physical or mental handicaps.
Their parents were preparing them to make the most of their abilities,
and envisaged them moving into some sort of sheltered living, at an
appropriate time, with the family continuing to play an important back-
up role. In one case, however, the siblings had made it plain to their
parents that they would not take on responsibility for their adopted

brother when the parents were no longer able to do so. This family also saw themselves as playing a diminishing role in the life of the youngster whom they still felt unable to love:

> Adoptive mother: "All we can look forward to is getting him as independent as we can and see that he finishes up in an establishment where he can get the best out of his abilities. It just sort of jogs. I can't survive unless I take one day at a time."

In contrast, as evidence of the importance of the extended family in providing a "family for life", another foster mother of mentally handicapped teenage brothers said:

> "It's the fact that we're a large family which has saved us. Our oldest son [aged 20 still living at home] is really marvellous with them. We've often said if we'd been on our own, we wouldn't have coped. If you've had to fight all your life, you don't give up easily. If we give up, where do they go from here? That could sound as if nobody else in the world could look after them - I don't believe that. But I can see that they are beginning to be able to cope. When they move away, there will be always somebody in this family to keep an eye on them."

Were the members of the new family satisfied with the placement?

As with attachment, this question was considered in the context of the children themselves, the mother, the father, and the other children in the household.

Were the children satisfied?

We were unable to talk to four children, and a fifth was too mentally handicapped to express an opinion, but our main source of evidence for the others is the children or young people themselves. The comments of the parents, social workers, and the reports have been used to allow an estimate of whether the other five would have been likely to feel satisfied. We found that the youngsters all had something positive to say about their experience of growing up in a new family. Even the youngster who was adrift on his own said that his social worker had definitely done the right thing to place him with that family:

> "Oh yes, I'm very glad I went there, oh yes. Most of the time I felt I belonged. Part of the time I didn't feel I ought to have been there. It was my sister's attitude. My Mum and Dad always made me feel I ought to have been there. Some other foster children came. I was glad they came. They were better off there than where they were before. I had a home there. Why shouldn't anybody else? I feel as if I'm adopted. The only difference is it didn't go through the court. Everyone around here knows me as a Jackson."

One lad, placed at eleven, said more positively:

> "I'm as well off as any of my friends. If I'm at work, I'm not ashamed to say I'm fostered."

It was estimated that 14 of the youngsters were completely satisfied, and three were satisfied with some reservations (81 per cent), Four were fairly satisfied, but had serious reservations, and none were totally dissatisfied. All those who had serious reservations were over eleven at placement. Two said that they had doubts because of relationships within the family, whilst the other two had not particularly wanted to move to a new family, and thought that they would have done just as well had they stayed in the Children's Home. When I asked a 17-year old member of a sibling group if she was glad she had come, she said: "Yeah - I'm not too sure. I feel - I don't really know." She went on to tell me that she had enjoyed the Children's Home, and couldn't understand why people didn't think Children's Homes were a good place to be.

Another youngster of a similar age had very mixed feelings. Looking back at the time of interview, from the safety of her own place, she said that yes, she had hated the Children's Home, and was glad that the social worker had brought her to Norfolk. However, she said that most of the time she had been unhappy, and if social workers had asked her, she would have asked them to take her away. She was now glad that they had not done so.

When I asked a 14-year old whether the social workers had done the right thing, he replied:

"In a way yes, and in a way no. Yes, because it makes me feel happier being here, but I miss my own family. If I hadn't come it would have gone off worse. I can see my family every so often."

He said the saddest time of his life was when his mother died, and the next saddest time was when he had to leave his father. He then said:

"Tell Anne [his social worker] I'm pleased I came here. She helped me in this life, and I used to have dinner in her office. I liked her."

From his parents' description of his behaviour and, indeed, from the tension and anxiety to please which came through in the interview, it was considered that this youngster was not giving a totally accurate picture of his feelings. When asked what the good things were about the placement he said, "My own bedroom." When asked what the most unhappy times were, he said, "I haven't got any. It's all overcome." But when asked what the less good things were about living there, he insisted that the tape-recorder was turned off before talking of the trouble he got into for telling lies, and of his confusion about why he did this.

One 14-year old was completely satisfied with the placement, but still regretted that it had been necessary, and that his birth family had not wanted him:

"After about the first year, I thought this is a fine old place, I think I'll stay here. When my social worker said, what would I like, I told her somebody who'd like me. The first year was more or less the happiest year. I remember Mum was very nice to me, and still is. Occasionally we fall out - don't we, Mum? Just lately - I don't know why it is - I keep having dreams - I wonder what my Mum's doing now, how my Dad's doing, what my sisters are doing."

Was the mother satisfied?

There were lower satisfaction rates for members of the new families. Eleven of the mothers were completely satisfied, and another five were fairly satisfied but with some reservations, giving a satisfaction rate for mothers of 76 per cent. Four had serious reservations and one was not at all satisfied. Those parents of older children who were able to gain satisfaction from what the social worker described as "parenting in a different way", were more likely to be satisfied, as were those who, like the parents described by Hornby (1986), were able to take pleasure from the positives, and distance themselves from the more negative aspects of the children's behaviour.

In our earlier study it was hypothesised (Thoburn et al., 1986) that success was likely to be related to whether the motivations of the families for taking a youngster matched the needs of the children, and what the children were able to give back. There was evidence to support this view at the five-year stage also. Those who had taken a youngster in order to complete their family, such as childless couples, could not disguise their disappointment when an older youngster had not become fully attached to them; on the other hand those whose motivation was essentially altruistic needed to find some way of believing that they had actually been helpful to the youngsters. A family who had taken a youngster partly for altruistic reasons but also to complete their own family said:

"I think we've a lot to do, and a long way to go, but I think it's just a matter of time. Certainly, I feel it's been successful in that we _are_ a family. I judge success by feeling that we are a family. No, we don't regret it, not at all."

The adoptive parents of the youngster who turned out to be more mentally handicapped than they had expected said, with pride:

"His school report said he's a real character at school, much loved by everybody. There's no comparing what he is now and what he was then. He's picking-up quickly. We are his family. We don't even think he's adopted. He feels as if he's always been with us."

They were able to see progress in small things, and their ambition for him was that he should learn to speak.

Those whose motives had been essentially altruistic were able to feel satisfaction even though the youngsters had not become attached to them, and still had serious problems. One mother, who had herself been unhappily fostered as a child, said that she had felt it had all been worth it when she was approached by a neighbour who had recently had a handicapped baby:

"My neighbour said - 'I look at their quality of life and I know that my son has a future'. Just a little thing like that did make me feel good. I could see that others could see their quality of life is pretty good. I didn't expect it to be such a struggle as it has been. I don't think we are such a relaxed family as we used to be. So it has done us some harm. My work makes a difference. I think I've survived because I've got so many interests. They don't appear to be able to give much back in any way. Because we are all very different in our family, they should be able to respond to some if not all of us, but they seem to be totally unable to. Nobody will ever know how much they have cost us. They've cost us hundreds of pounds. They are still so destructive. We tend to think this is part and parcel of what you have to expect. I'm not saying we regret it. If I'd known, we wouldn't have taken it on. We've often said - I don't like saying it but that's a fact - we wished we'd taken on two children that really would have appreciated it. Two other children would have benefitted much more than these. I think they were in need. They also treated us like a Children's Home, and they've never wanted it to be more than that. I think by now there should have been some sign that they were a part of our family. I personally believe that this is something we were able to do - even when I've felt dreadful I've felt that at the end of it, I've sat down and thought about it, we've done right. I know they've benefitted. I know that so many things have happened that wouldn't have happened in the Children's Home. But it's not give and take. They can't give anything."

Three families who had taken youngsters who had not been able to become fully attached had made the point that perhaps they could have helped more with children who were more able to respond to the love they had to give.

Were the fathers satisfied?

Thirteen (62 per cent) of the fathers were completely or fairly satisfied, with four having serious reservations, and four being totally dissatisfied, including the foster father whose marriage broke up and who was no longer in contact with the youngster concerned. The comments of fathers were very similar to those of the mothers, although they were less likely to gain satisfaction from the little things which helped their wives to keep going. More of the fathers thought that the youngsters would have been just as well off had they stayed in their Children's Homes.

> Foster father: "It was a different kind of love to what I expected. Not like you'd expect of an adopted son. I did love him enough to think he'd always be there. He wanted a Mum and Dad. But what did he want us for? As a Mum and Dad? Or as somebody he can use at a time when he is in trouble? I don't think he would have been a lot worse off if he'd stayed in the Children's Home. A relationship with a residential worker would have been as good as us."

In at least three cases marriages were threatened:

> Adoptive father: "She [his wife] was murder to live with for eighteen months."

> Adoptive mother: "I would have left with Jenny [youngest child] and that would have been it. I thought if I left, he [husband] would have to do something about getting him out. I got a job instead. We didn't row over it. It doesn't rest with the man of the household. It's the woman who takes the full thrust."

Adoptive father: "In fact that strained our relationship for a while. It wasn't just our relationship with each other, but with our children. He could have broken up our family. It was getting a very big strain."

On the other hand, some fathers gained great satisfaction from the arrival of the youngster as part of their family, and this involved those who had taken handicapped babies as well as those who had taken older children.

Foster father of 17 year old: "When I come in at night, I look around and look forward to seeing him. He's the one who says - 'dad, have you had a good day?'"

Were the siblings satisfied?

There were natural or adoptive siblings in the homes into which 12 children moved. Only half of these were either completely or fairly satisfied. It was usually because of their own children that parents were inclined to be dissatisfied.

Adoptive mother: "We have been wrong to do it - adopt - because of the effect it had on our own children. I may have done a very good thing for him, but I certainly haven't done a very good thing for our own children. I feel guilty about this, which doesn't help. Our daughter will blame us for adopting him for the rest of her life. He pushed her out of the home too soon. It would have been easier on our own children if he'd been fostered. The family sees adoption as having another brother and now they don't like him they feel guilty. If it's fostering, they make more allowances. If it's adoption, they don't make allowances."

A social worker said of another family:

"It's been too big a price to pay - for them and their own children."

Interestingly, and contrary to findings in other studies, (see, for example, Trasler, 1960 and Parker, 1966), all those families who took on a youngster in part as a companion for their own child found that their plans worked well.

Adoptive father: "It's been very successful for our daughter. More than anything else, she has a marvellous time with him. She's been wonderful to and about him right from the start. She's always given to him, shared with him. She's tremendously protective and supportive of him. More than we are."

This impression of closeness between them was certainly confirmed when we interviewed these two youngsters together. In those cases where older children had attached quickly to the newcomers, they had benefitted by the fact that their parents were more able to allow them to move towards independence as they were preoccupied with their new child.

It was interesting to note that, like Festinger (1986), we found that children did less well if placed as a single boy or girl in a family where all the siblings were of the opposite sex and where one of the reasons for taking the child was to have a child of a different sex.

Were the placements "successful"?

In making an overall assessment of success most weight has been placed on those indicators such as "a family for life", which seem most to capture the original intention of those initiating permanence policies.

Table 3 shows that 16 (76 per cent) were very successful or successful, and if the "fairly successful but some reservations" category is included there would be a success rate of 86 per cent of the children placed. If, however, one adds those not placed, 62 per cent of the first 29 children referred were successfully placed by the project. Table 4 summarises success rates in terms of the different indicators used.

Table 3
Overall success of 21 children five years after placement
(global rating of researcher)

Very Successful		Successful		Fairly Successful*		Serious Reservations		Unsuccessful	
No.	%	No.	%	No.	%	No.	%	No.	%
7	33	9	43	2	10	2	10	1	5

*some reservations

69

Table 4

Indicators of success in permanent family placement of 29 children
(21 placed) five years after placement/referral

	YES No.	%	NO No.	%
Was the child placed?	21	72	8	28
Did the placement last for 5 years? (No includes 2 who left at 17 but were still in touch)	19	90	2	10
Was the child adopted?	16	76	5	24
Did the child have a "sense of permanence"?	20	95	1	5
Did the parents have a "sense of permanence"?	21	100	-	-
Did the child have a sense of personal identity?	16	76	5	24
Were there no serious concerns about the child's well-being?	14	67	7	33
Did the child's well-being improve? (Yes includes 3 whose well-being was high before placement and remained so)	16	76	5	24
Was at least one parent well attached to child?	18	85	3	15
Was the child well attached to at least one parent?	14	67	7	33
Had the child found "a family for life"?	19	90	2	10
Was the child satisfied with the placement?	17	81	4	19
Was the mother satisfied with the placement?	16	76	5	24
Was the father satisfied with the placement?	13	62	8	38
Were the natural children of the family satisfied? (12 placements only)	6	50	6	50
Was the placement successful? (overall rating of researcher)	18	86	3	14
What proportion of those referred were placed successfully?	18	62	11	38

70

SOME CONCLUDING REMARKS ABOUT THE QUALITATIVE STUDY

The findings from this study have been presented in terms of different measures of success, but could equally well have been divided in terms of the different sources of evidence. It is interesting to note that relying on the evidence of the children and young people would have produced a higher success rate, whilst reliance on objective tests such as well-being and behaviour would have led to a lower estimate. In response to the question as to whether the placement was a success, parents and social workers often answered in terms of success for whom?

> Foster father: "It's been a disaster from the family's point of view. From his point of view, he'll have made more progress physically than he would have done somewhere else. That's all that's going for him. There's nothing going for us."

Two explanations come to mind for the generally more positive rating of the young people. Some of those in their early teens felt very happy that they were a part of their new family, especially as they could remember the traumas and separations of the past; others, even if they felt uncertainty, would have been unlikely to express it - given their desperate need to hang on to the good bits of the placement.

The youngsters in their late teens, on the other hand, seemed to be going through a phase of living for the moment. Whether they were happily settled in their families, or were somewhat adrift, they still talked in terms of the here and now, their friendships, their work situation. Their definition of happiness seemed to be very different from that of their parents. Thus, a youngster who was pregnant, practically homeless, in serious financial difficulty, and about to go to court for about the fifth time, said:

> "I'm a lot happier now 'cos I'm doing what I want to do. I don't know what I'd be doing now if I'd gone to another kids home."

When asked if she had any problems, she said:

> "No. I'm still in lots of bother with the police but I ain't bothering about it."

The former foster parents of one lad thought that he had a drink problem. Asked if he had any problems about drink, he said:

> "Drink - it's not a problem. I just enjoy a drink like most people do. I haven't got a drink problem. It's probably what Mum and Dad think. I'm alright. Tell my social worker everything's alright. I don't think I need a social worker any more. He might think I need him, but I don't."

When asked if he had any difficulties, he said:

> "Yes, getting a job. Apart from that, everything's OK. I have more friends than I've ever had. I haven't really got an ambition, just to do as well as possible, that's all. I should think this is probably the happiest time I've ever had."

71

This optimistic phase in the lives of these youngsters, which probably extends into their 20s, does give rise to questions about interviews with young adults about their satisfaction with the growing up experience as the major source of evidence about success. It is interesting in this respect that many of the people contacting Post-Adoption Centres seem to be in their middle years, a time when questions about identity seem more likely to come to the fore again.

Before concluding this section it is appropriate to return to the question of the purpose of permanent family placement. At the heart of this policy lies the assumption that "ordinary families" can take in children who have special needs as part of their families, and that the continuity, stability, good-parenting, and sense of belonging, which will come from this experience will be enough to help them overcome, or at least cope with, their handicap, or their earlier deprivation. The emphasis is on love and family life, and not on treatment although some permanent foster or adoptive families do become skilled helpers as well. When considering younger children, whether or not they have mental or physical disabilities, there is much in the research to support this view. The older the youngster, however, the more questions arise, both as far as the welfare of the children is concerned and also the well-being of the "ordinary families" who take them in. This chapter has given evidence of some of the costs to the families themselves, and also to some of the children who described usually quite short, but sometimes prolonged, periods of unhappiness, stress and strain in trying to fit in. Although the names of specialist placement agencies - "The Child Wants a Home", "Parents for Children" or "Children Need Families" - seem to stress that it is the child's needs which are paramount, once a child is placed with a permanent new family, it is the child who has to adjust to fit in with the family. This is in contrast to the position of children placed in therapeutic establishments, whether "professional" foster placements or group care settings. Bettelheim's phrase "love is not enough" exemplifies this different way of thinking, whereby the regime for a youngster is planned around that youngster's needs.

Our conversations with parents were peppered with phrases such as "he was alright once we'd got him into our way of thinking". Similar themes are in evidence in the articles by or about adoptive parents of "special needs" children in a recent book on post-placement support (Argent, 1988). This is no criticism. It is, indeed, what permanent family placement is about. Nevertheless, some of the social workers had to stand back, and - having decided that the needs of the youngster were most likely to be met by permanent placement with an "ordinary family" - watch the parents handle situations in ways which their therapeutic instincts and knowledge did not support. Families and social workers were aware of this.

Foster father: "We disagreed about the way to handle the smoking. Patricia might say - buy her 10 a week. We'd say we've never done that with our own and we aren't going to start with her. I'd tell her that I respected her views. She never went against us. When you've brought a family up, and I think I get on well with youngsters, get control over them, you go your own way, don't you? You get advice and that. Our method had worked with the boy but it didn't work with her. Perhaps, if we'd bought her the cigarettes and let her stay out 'til three in the morning - but all the people who come round here - there wasn't one that disagreed with us. But I've got to say her time here wasn't very nice for us or for her."

Foster mother: "We've been very strict with them. But I'm positive that underneath this has been good for them. I'm a believer in firm discipline. A certain amount of security goes with that. I don't think the social workers have interfered with us, but I've had the impression, been given the impression, many times, that we've got it all wrong. But I know we can go anywhere with these two boys. And within reason they'll behave themselves. The school was a tremendous hindrance. There was no discipline there. They were happy there - to be fair to the school."

Social worker: "Permanence means allowing families to do it _their_ way. But they may miss out on the "treatment" which a different placement might have given them. If fitting-in is the main thing, other things may have to go."

In the Chapter which follows, the focus moves to a consideration of some of the implications of this review of the costs and benefits of permanent family placement for the social workers who make the decisions and provide support to the children and their new families.

5 The social workers' contribution to the success of the placements

So far the focus has been on the evaluation of permanent substitute family placement and not on the role of the social workers in helping to maintain children in placement. However, those interviewed for the qualitative study had much to say about the contribution to success (or otherwise) of the social workers. Fanshel and Shinn (1978) and Aldgate (1980) concluded that the activities of social workers did make a difference to whether children returned home from care or not. Though it cannot be demonstrated statistically because of the small numbers, the comments of parents and the workers themselves suggest that they played a crucial role in supporting some of the families through difficult patches which might well have ended in disruption. It has been suggested elsewhere (Thoburn and Rowe, 1988) that differential rates of breakdown amongst placements made by voluntary agencies surveyed, and by some local authorities, may be in part accounted for by different social work practice before and after placement.

Social workers placing children with permanent new families have two major roles: finding the families and making appropriate placements; and supporting the new families after placement. In our earlier study (Thoburn et al., 1986), we considered in some detail the nature of social work practice in the early stages of placement, and particularly the delicate art of collaborating with others in the interests of the children and families. Space precludes a detailed analysis of the social work service, but some of the more general conclusions are considered here which have either been strengthened by a consideration of the placements at the five-year stage, or which are relevant to practice at the later stages of placement.

74

The model of practice followed by workers at The Child Wants a Home, which is similar to that of other permanent placement units in Britain and the States, can best be characterised as an "empowerment" or "participatory" model. (See Maluccio et al., 1986, and Thoburn, 1988 for a fuller discussion of the principles which underlie this style of work.) In our earlier report we described social work after placement in terms of consultation:

> The parents wanted, and for the most part received, the sort of service which a social worker asks of a team leader. They accepted the workers' ultimate authority, but had confidence that the authority delegated to them as parents would not be interfered with unless this was necessary in the interest of the child. Reassurred by this, they wanted regular opportunities to describe their activities, explain their difficulties, explore their ideas for alternative ways of handling them, consider other suggestions and receive offers of help in any joint work to be done. They wanted to share their happy moments and successes, receive praise and share pleasure. For this to happen they needed to feel valued and for all members of the family to be cared about. Finally, they needed to know that in a crisis competent help would be speedily available to them. (Thoburn et al., 1986, p.170).

MAKING THE PLACEMENT

It will be immediately apparent that if an empowerment model of social work is to be used social workers must feel confident that the original placement is right. The work of the project in the early stages was characterised by meticulous and skilled work, based on practice wisdom, and on a sound knowledge of law, child development, and social work practice with children and families.

Decisions had to be taken about whether a particular child was really wanting a new family and able to make the effort which would be required of him or her in order to fit in; about whether a family offering to take a special needs child had the skills and resilience to do so; and whether a particular family could parent a particular child or sibling group. Workers also had to decide about which legal route to permanence was appropriate for each child; what the degree of contact should be with important people from the past, especially birth parents and siblings, and whether the legal option appropriate for the child was in keeping with the aspirations of the new family. Such decisions had to be taken co-operatively, and the work shared with a range of individuals and organisations. These included the local authority social workers, seniors, and adoption panels of the agencies responsible for the children, the court, especially if the youngster was a ward of court, and, of course, all members of the new families, the natural parents, and the children themselves. (See especially Morris, 1984, on the importance of listening carefully to what the youngsters have to say).

Looking back from the vantage point of five years on, the finding that 90 per cent of the children had found a "family for life", and that none of the children was totally dissatisfied with the experience of living with their new family, would suggest that the model of practice and particularly the choice of placements was generally successful. Sifting through the less positive comments, however, doubts which were expressed in the first report as to whether the range of routes to permanence was adequately utilised in order to meet the needs of the youngsters remain. At that stage, the view was expressed that some of the youngsters accepted on referral but later withdrawn could have been placed with the substitute families they clearly needed if the question of adoption had been kept open so that they could make up their own minds once settled in the placement, perhaps with the opportunity of continuing contact with their birth families. We recommended that workers discussing substitute family placement with youngsters should talk in terms of "a permanent new family", or "a family for life" rather than in terms of "adoption", in order to avoid the disappointment which was already being expressed by some of the youngsters at the two-year stage, or the stresses on children and parents which resulted from agonising over whether and when the adoption application should be made.

Whilst small numbers must still counsel caution, the finding that 95 per cent of the youngsters had a strong or fairly strong sense of permanence, irrespective of whether they were fostered or adopted, is at least consistent with Lahti's finding from a larger study (1982) that a sense of permanence and not necessarily legal permanence should be the aim. Such a policy might well result in more children in care allowing themselves to be placed with permanent substitute families.

On the issue of contact with birth families, there was no evidence that such contact was detrimental to the placements. In the one case where this was a real issue, it was admitted by all concerned that the youngster would certainly not have allowed himself to be placed had contact been terminated. One cannot simply wish away inconvenient facts, and especially feelings expressed by youngsters at the stage of decision-making. Morris (1984, p.18) was critical of a "tendency towards omnipotence", on the part of those preparing youngsters for placement, and concluded: "In the rush for security the child's needs for continuity with his family may be lost, and his identity shattered."

The lower success rate if measured in terms of a sense of identity, together with the evidence from some of the youngsters about the stresses they experienced in trying to squeeze themselves into being the person their new parents wanted them to be, does lend support to Morris's thesis. It must be admitted, however, that deciding whether to go ahead with a "linking" must be the most difficult of tasks and that the majority of youngsters, some of whom we would not have expected to fit into their new families, took on new identities with which they seemed to be totally comfortable.

It is worth noting that three of the children whose outcomes were less than totally satisfactory had initially said that they did not want a new family to be found for them. Whilst in later interviews each insisted that their social workers had done the right thing, our findings would suggest that when youngsters are uncertain at the initial stages, careful thought must be given to the form of permanence chosen for them, and the way in which the new families are prepared. Powell (1983), who interviewed in depth 17 young people who had been adopted as older children, found support for his hypothesis that "more choice, more preparation, and participation" on the part of the young person would lead to "a greater tendency for closeness with the adoptive family ... and to a greater reconciliation with the past as manifested in less uneasiness and more well-being" (p.91).

The project workers interviewed about their perceptions of the success of the placements made comments which also fitted with this hypothesis. Like Powell, and Triseliotis and Russell (1984) they concluded from their own experience that children in the right environment did have the capacity to recover from early traumatic experiences. One worker, when asked for his measure of success, said:

"The children are mature and realise some at least of their various potentials so that they are able to lead independent lives - by the time they reach 18 for a girl, perhaps a bit more, say 20, for a boy. That they have satisfying relationships and a sense of identity, and are generally enjoying their lives. I think the fact that these exist is based on the security of having a family for life. Young people wouldn't recognise this quality of having a family for life, because of the age they are, but I think it's a bedrock that they have which they take for granted. All have the potential. Some take a long time to get there. Good nurturing speeds things up, bad nurturing holds them back."

This worker and his colleagues commented on the special problems of children placed at around ten and older, especially in terms of the short time available to families to provide a nurturing experience so that the youngsters could move on to emotional and physical independence.

Social worker: "The time span is so short between a 10-year old arriving and becoming a teenager. I would think twice about placing an older child with a childless couple."

Speaking of one of the youngsters who had felt constrained by the requirement to fit in with the new family, another worker said:

"She's typical of a syndrome. You get these children late - you do your best for them. They are immature. They have to burst their way out of the family. She made a mess of life, but she never lost contact. Her foster mother will go on being there for her."

It is important not to lose sight of the lower satisfaction rate amongst the members of the new families, and to consider whether the findings may offer suggestions about improving this situation. It would seem that parents taking older children must be prepared for the fact that children placed when older are unlikely to identify totally with their new family's way of doing things. Some will do so, but the majority will not. Some will become fully attached, but the majority will not commit themselves totally to the members of their new families. The ability to accept the difference between parenting a child who joins the family later, and parenting a biological child or one who joins the family in infancy or as a toddler, may well be the most important indicator of whether families are successfully able to undertake the enterprise of taking an older child permanently into their family.

The findings outlined in Chapter 4, and those of other research studies, suggest that if these differences are accepted, and if a range of routes to permanence is used, permanent family placement can be successful for the majority of children in care unable to return to their birth families, and for whom "shared care" is inappropriate. However, the comments of some of the parents, and the youngsters themselves, did suggest that for a small minority, the concept of permanent substitute family placement was stretched too far. We have seen that the essence of such policies is to place youngsters with "ordinary families" possibly at the expense of offering more specialised treatment, or the acceptance of a youngster's own special identity. Some parents also considered that because of their early distressing and damaging experiences the youngsters placed with them were unable to accept the love which they had to offer, and to return it. It may well be that these youngsters would have been more appropriately placed in "permanent" situations, whether small group care settings or larger foster families of the non-traditional family type, where there was more potential for planning a regime particularly suited to their needs, and which was more able to respect their personal identity. This is not to criticise the parents who gave so much to them, but to question whether too high a price was paid by the children and families for the benefits of "ordinary family" living, both in terms of the lost opportunity to offer more appropriate help to the youngsters, and the stresses and strains which the natural children of the host families were obliged to endure. At least three of the families had come to this conclusion.

This would suggest that at the assessment stage, models of permanence which do not involve placement with families with the intention that the parents will take on the full substitute parenting role, should also be considered. It would, however, be essential for such families, or group care staff, to be willing, and enabled by their management structures, to play a continuing role in the youngsters' lives once they had reached eighteen. Such a policy would be in line with the recommendations of Mann (1984) and Stein and Carey (1986) drawn from their interviews with young people who had left care. Regrettably, most professional fostering schemes do not accept that permanent relationships may be formed, and therefore do not find ways of nurturing such relationships although they may be essential in providing vital support to the youngsters as they move into adult life.

THE SOCIAL WORK ROLE IN SUPPORTING THE PLACEMENTS

Looking back over the five years, the success of most of the placements would appear to justify the model of practice which involved transferring the maximum amount of power to the new families. One may at least hypothesise that it was this way of working which allowed a sense of permanence to develop even for those who remained as foster children for periods of years before adoption, or who were not adopted. It may help to explain why the findings about a sense of permanence are at variance with those of researchers, including Triseliotis (1983), Triseliotis and Hill (1988), and Rowe and her colleagues (1984), who have studied populations of long-term foster children supervised using more traditional methods which emphasise the role of the local authority.

In reporting on this style of work at the two-year stage, it was noted that risks were taken by the workers in operating in a way which differs in important respects from what is usually considered to be good practice with foster children. In particular, they could have been open to criticism for not working directly with the children and spending time with them on their own. As social workers, children, and parents talked about the preceding five years, it became apparent that things could have gone badly wrong, and that an official inquiry might have found fault with this departure from accepted practice. It is rare in these days of child abuse inquiries for hindsight to be used to commend work undertaken, and to show that the risks taken were justified in terms of successful outcome.

The majority of families accepted the power delegated to them and got on, in their own way, with knitting themselves together as new families. Some, especially those taking younger children, proceeded quite quickly to adoption, and made little use of the social work services which would have been available had they needed them. They still enjoyed coming to the annual "family days", to show off their youngsters and receive praise for the progress made, and were further reinforced in their sense of self-worth when invited as "veterans" to talk to potential new parents. Some also made use of the post-adoption services offered by the agency and attended study days, for example, on telling Down's youngsters about adoption, or on helping black children placed with white families to retain a sense of their cultural identity and to cope with racism.

Some spoke rather wistfully, and at times reproachfully, of the fact that the social workers seemed to lose interest in them once the child had been adopted. This was not because they needed help, but because they had grown to feel affection for the worker, and wanted to go on sharing their sense of achievement and pleasure with the person who had been so important in the early days of the placement. It was hard for them to understand, or to accept, that they could matter to the workers before the adoption hearing, and then be forgotten soon afterwards. If these parents did need support or services, they turned to their families, to the services available to non-adoptive families, and to self-help groups such as the Down's Association in which they often played significant roles.

Three of the families who adopted asked for social work help after the adoption, in one case returning to the agency for a brief counselling session which they found helpful, in one case drawing in the agency and the local authority area social worker and in a third case choosing the local authority social worker, and not contacting the agency.

Ten children, including these three adopted youngsters, continued to require social work services well into the third, fourth or fifth years of placement, two requiring merely supervisory services because they remained foster children, but eight needing more extensive social work inputs.

By the 3-year stage, a sense of permanence had already been established as a result of the social workers' emphasis on the authority of the new parents. Families were functioning as "ordinary families", or at least as "reconstituted" families and were less conscious of their adoptive or foster family status. They wanted this status to be acknowledged by anyone offering them help, but not to be constantly used as an explanation for the youngsters' problems, or an excuse for inappropriate behaviour.

After the first two or three years in the more difficult placements, social workers took a higher profile with the youngsters, and could do so without unduly threatening the sense of permanence. This was more appropriate than at the start of the placement in that several were by this stage young adults and beginning to need a service in their own right, especially in those cases where personal identity may have suffered in the interests of finding a niche in the new family.

Parents were still looking to social workers to reinforce their parental role, and complained bitterly when workers chatted to youngsters about how good they were at football, instead of asking them why they had been thieving from the village shop, and how they proposed to improve their behaviour. In two cases this reinforcement of parental authority involved workers in making it clear to youngsters that they would be placed away from the home if their behaviour did not improve. Such a threat in the early stages of placement would almost certainly have led to breakdown, whereas at the later stage it was seen as a realistic statement of the position. Fortunately both these lads were able to think things over and decide that concessions had to be made in the interests of their remaining in the place which had become home to them.

Six of the youngsters had some form of respite care, or a brief "cooling-off" period away from the home. For two children this was built into the placement from the beginning, but the other parents had varying degrees of difficulty in asking for such help in the later stages of placement. For two it was made easier because the children had mental or physical handicaps which made such requests respectable even though the real reason was emotional or behavioural difficulties rather than disability. It should be noted that, unlike the natural parents described by Packman (1986) and Fisher et al. (1986), these families were usually offered respite care quickly and willingly, rather than grudgingly, and with recriminations. In one case where there was a long delay in looking for lodgings for a teenager, the parents considered that this led to the irretrievable rupture of the relationships which might otherwise have continued:

> Foster mother: "I don't think he could believe how bad it was getting. I said, 'Will you please move him soon. I don't want to put him on the doorstep.'"

This finding is in line with that of the larger scale American studies referred to earlier of Nelson (1985) and Hornby (1986), and emphasises the importance of building the possibility of respite care into social work services to families taking "special needs" children.

Despite the strong family therapy orientation of one of the workers, and the use of family therapy techniques in the home study and approval stages, therapeutic approaches were rarely viewed as appropriate by children or parents. Some parents wanted the youngsters to be referred as individuals to family psychiatry departments, but the youngsters resisted this strongly, refusing to be labelled as "cuckoo". Social workers supported them in this, and only referred for individual help if the youngsters were themselves asking for this. Family therapy was used for assessment or treatment purposes in five cases, but was perceived as helpful by the youngster and family in only one case. Most parents felt that this approach implied that there was something wrong with them as a family, whereas their perception of the situation was that they were a normally healthy family who had run into difficulties because of the arrival in their midst of a particularly damaged child.

On the whole, then, the "house style" of offering support to the parents was continued into the later stages of placement, with a higher profile being taken with adolescents. The most appropriate way of characterising this later work would be in terms of conciliation as described by Parkinson (1987) rather than in terms of any particular therapeutic model. Thus, the youngsters' comments about social work visits varied from:

17-year old foster child: "I never really see them. They never really say anything - except if it's gone bad, and it's never gone bad".

When asked about his reviews he said they didn't bother him, he went once and he really didn't care either way. In contrast, Mary, aged 17, said:

"The social workers helped quite a bit. We used to have family arguments. I was glad to see the back of them, though."

Workers continued to help some of the youngsters to keep in contact with members of birth families. For three youngsters who had left home, and for three still in placement, but who were moving towards independent living, they were teachers of social skills, providers of money when eviction from digs loomed large, and conciliators when this was needed.

Adoptive mother: "He would talk to us first, and then the children. Then all together. When you'd got both sides of the story, it needed someone to bring them together. That's all you need sometimes - a referee."

Social worker: "The parents would never agree to family meetings, though I did manage a few. But they were counter-productive because Jim got so angry. They would agree to negotiating style meetings but not to therapy style meetings. That was much safer. One has to try to find something that works. With the older youngsters it's a mixture of support and counselling."

One indicator of success mentioned by some (though not the project workers) is "closing the case", or "getting the family off the books". Whilst this aim is to be applauded in that there is a risk that long-term social work may create unnecessary dependence, and become less effective, (see especially Sainsbury et al., 1982), it was not included as an indicator of success as it does not relate to the needs of the youngsters or families. Had it been, the success rate would have been quite low as 43 per cent were still needing a social work service five years after placement. Lynch and Roberts (1982) have shown that abused children may be "taken off the books" but this does not necessarily mean that they are no longer in need of services, and indeed they noted that several of the children who had been abused and were considered presumably no longer to need a service were indeed still in emotional distress, or in need of remedial services. Our finding that both social work and services were still needed for either prolonged or intermittent periods is in line with other studies (notably Nelson, 1985), and the conclusions of practitioners (Argent, 1988). They suggest that those who are turning towards permanent family placement as a means of "getting families off the books" will not achieve this aim, at least in respect of a fair proportion of older children. The comments of parents and children would suggest that a style of social work which avoids the pitfalls of long-term practice identified by Sainsbury and his colleagues, but which does not leave vulnerable youngsters, and families without help, would resemble the "preventive maintenance" approach advocated by Jones (1985, p.143) as a result of her study of preventive and rehabilitative services to vulnerable families:

> The implications of such an approach are that intensity can rise and fall based on the needs of the case; the service boundaries are permeable so families can easily enter, and leave, and re-enter; and the emphasis of the service program is upon 'being there', providing continuity, and serving as a resource to the family, rather than upon providing a time-limited, goal-oriented service and closing the case.

Maluccio and his colleagues (1985) suggest that the "empowerment" model should reduce the risks of creating unnecessary dependence:

> Empowering parents by means of carefully constructed agreements, in which they fully participate, and by involving them in case conferences so that they may have the information which helps to combat a sense of powerlessness, is a major part of the strategy to prevent unnecessary dependence or a sense of victimisation. Parents need to be asked if they are satisfied with the way things are progressing. Are there services they would like changed? Is there a different kind of help they would like? (p.146).

These comments about appropriate models of practice for families under stress are not inappropriate when referring to adoptive or foster families and, indeed, could be a description of the service offered by the Children's Society and by other progressive agencies; (see, for example, Hutton's account of the work of the Lothian Adopters' Group and its relationship with the specialist social workers (Argent, 1988)). Looking back over the third, fourth and fifth years of the placements, the comments of the new families about the services needed and those offered were very similar to those made to other researchers by natural families (see, especially Thoburn, 1980; Fisher et al., 1986; Packman, 1986). In some areas permanence policies have already had a beneficial effect on social work practice with families whose children return to them from care, by introducing new methods of working which have been developed in the context of work with substitite families. Life story work, for example, may be just as necessary for a youngster moving back to a "reconstituted" family. On the principle of enlisting "the sharp elbows of the middle-classes" espoused by Frank Field when leading the Child Poverty Action Group campaign for higher Family Allowances, it is just possible that social workers will hear the criticism of the services they offer to families under stress if they come from "deserving" new families, after having, for many years, ignored comments made to researchers by natural families about the kind of service they would find helpful.

6 Conclusion – some pointers for fututre research

In Chapter 4 extensive use was made of the words of children and parents as they described their aspirations, pleasures and problems in coming together as new families. Their views about the nature of success informed a critique of the different indicators which have been used to research the effectiveness of permanent substitute family placement of children with special needs. Whatever indicator is chosen, the review of the evaluative literature, and the detailed study, indicate that permanence policies are achieving results in which their authors can take some pride. However, more research is needed as there are still many questions to be answered.

It was noted in Chapter 2 that findings on the characteristics of people who can successfully parent other peoples' children are inconclusive or contradictory. On the other hand, large and small-scale studies agree broadly about the characteristics of children who are more likely to succeed in substitute foster or adoptive families. The quantitative and qualitative studies of the work of British permanent placement agencies confirm earlier findings on the relationship between age at placement and success, with higher rates of breakdown for older children.

From these studies it seems that it is now necessary to break down the "hard-to-place" groups into those who are younger, and have some form of physical or mental handicap, and those who are older, whose problems are more likely to lie in behaviour disturbance, or learning difficulties. (Wedge and Mantle's forthcoming study of the placement of siblings, and Macaskill's (1985a) study of the placement of mentally handicapped youngsters are examples of the sorts of studies now needed, although controlling for age at placement will be important.) For the first group, the difficulty lies in finding the family, especially in doing so quickly enough for the disabled child to be offered consistent care in the positive environment provided by a loving family. For the children aged between five and ten, and for sibling groups, the problem is not so much that they are "hard-to-place" but that they may be hard to bring up. For children over the age of eleven, and some of those with mental handicaps under that age, the problem lies in their being both "hard-to-place" and "hard to bring up".

Previous failed attempts to settle into a new family, having been abused or neglected, and needing to stay in touch with important people from the past, also add to the difficulties. In fact, a list of the factors which make children difficult to place, and most at risk of breakdown, would apply to the majority of children in care needing permanent family placement. Agencies seeking to improve their success rates on the basis of research findings could easily do so by only accepting on referral those groups who are most easily placed - children under five, sibling groups in the younger age ranges, and handicapped babies. Such a course of action would leave permanence policies in tatters, since it would leave the majority of children in unplanned care. If such youngsters are to be offered homes with permanent new families, risks have to be taken. It therefore becomes the more important that lessons learned from the more successful agencies, such as the one we have described, are incorporated into practice.

Research on the placement of sub-groups of children may uncover explanations for the apparent discrepancies as to the sorts of families who can successfully parent children not born to them who have special needs. But necessary though these studies are in furthering understanding, special needs placement is likely to defy attempts at prediction. As Napier wrote in 1972, "children will continue to surprise us in their ability to make the most unexpected relationships, and in their refusal to conform to our pre-conceived ideas" (p.203).

As a case example of social work practice, the placement of children with special needs shows yet again that guidelines based on research and practice wisdom can be helpful but cannot replace the painstaking, and also intuitive, assessment of each case. Careful and adequately resourced work will cut down but not eliminate the risks, but can, as most of our youngsters and their new parents testified, bring rich rewards:

> Adoptive mother of Down's youngster: "No regrets? Oh, no. To say I never think about her not being ours wouldn't be true. I often think about it. She'll come up and say, 'I love you Mummy', and I feel so much love for her. You wouldn't think you could feel that love for a child you hadn't given birth to. I love her just as much as Mandy [natural daughter]. She is special in a different sort of way. Having a handicapped child gives you a different perspective on life completely. It re-orders your priorities."

84

PRINCIPAL EVALUATIVE STUDIES OF THE ADOPTION OR PERMANENT FOSTER
FAMILY PLACEMENT OF CHILDREN WITH 'SPECIAL NEEDS'

Author and Country	Size of sample	Type of study	Special Needs	Age at p'ment
Coyne & Brown 1985, USA	693	retro-spective	"developmentally disabled"	50% were of school age
Fanshel 1972 USA	395	retro-spective	American Indians mostly placed trans-racially	mostly under 5 years
Fein et al. 1983, USA	122	longi-tudinal	older children in care - deprived lives	2-12+ years
Festinger 1986, USA	897 and sub-group of 183	retro-spective	older children in care	1-16 yrs. average 4 yrs.
Fratter et al. 1982, UK	42	longi-tudinal "in house"	older children in care	avg. age 8 yrs.
Gill & Jackson 1983, UK (See also Raynor)	44 families	retro-spective	black or mixed parentage, mostly placed trans-racially	under 5

Type of p'ment	Time in placement at time of study	Definition of success and success rates
adoption by foster parents or "strangers"	12 months	9% disrupted. 18% of those aged 7+ at placement disrupted
adoption	most of childhood	Adoptive parents' accounts of adjustment. 75% problem free or making adequate adjustment. Older children at placement less well adjusted.
adoption by foster parents or "strangers"	12-16 months	91% of adopted and 50% of permanently fostered children still in placement. Well-being highest for those adopted by foster parents.
adoption by foster parents or "strangers"	1-4 yrs.	97% of children still in placement. 73% of parents rate own satisfaction as excellent or good.
adoption and permanent foster care with strangers	12-24 months	88% still in placement.
adoption	over 10 years	Interviews with parents and children. Assessment of well being. 83% of transracially placed assessed as successful.

Author and Country	Size of sample	Type of study	Special Needs	Age at p'ment
Grow & Shapiro 1974, 1975, USA	125	retro-spective	black or mixed parentage placed trans-racially	most under 5
Hart 1987, UK	172	retro-spective	general population of "special needs" children	most over 5 yrs. or sibling groups
Hoksbergen et al. 1987a, Holland	116	prospective/ longitudinal with control group	Thai children placed with Dutch families. Deprived early lives.	most under 5 yrs.
Hoksbergen et al. 1987b, Holland	16,000*	341 disrupted placements compared with non-disrupted	children from abroad; many with deprived backgrounds - most black	mostly under 5 yrs.

*approx. - all inter-country placements

Kadushin 1970, USA	91	retro-spective	older children	5-11 yrs.
Kagan & Reid 1986, USA	78	retro-spective	disturbed children in residential care	average 11 yrs.
Kaye & Tipton 1985, USA	all placed by 5 States	retro-spective*	general population of "special needs"	mostly older

*"special needs" children compared with other adopted children

Kerrane et al. 1982, UK	73	pros-pective "in-house"	children in care	mostly aged 5-9 yrs.

Type of p'ment	Time in placement at time of study	Definition of success and success rates
adoption	at least 7 years	Interviews with parents and children. Adjustment scales. 77% had adjusted satisfactorily.
adoption	1-5 years	95% still in placement.
adoption	5 years	Satisfaction of parents and behavioural checklists. 84% no reason for concern identified. Lower ratings for those older at placement.
adoption	varied	Admission to residential care taken to indicate disruption. 98% were not admitted to care. (69% of these which disrupted were over 6 at placement).
adoption	6-10 years	78% of parents satisfied or very satisfied.
adopted by "strangers"	5 years	71% adopted. 53% lasted five years. Well-being also assessed.
adoption	followed through to legal adoption or disruption	87% legally adopted. More disruptions amongst those over 12 at placement and emotionally handicapped.
adoption or permanent fostering	1-4 years	88% still in placement.

Author and Country	Size of sample	Type of study	Special Needs	Age at p'ment
Lahti 1982, USA	104	pros-pective	children in care	under 12 yrs.

*comparison group of children who went home

Author and Country	Size of sample	Type of study	Special Needs	Age at p'ment
Macaskill 1985a, 1988, UK	33	retro-spective	mentally handicapped	most under 5 yrs.
Nelson 1985, USA	257	retro-spective	handicapped or siblings	1-11+ years
O'Hara & Hoggan 1988, Scotland	335	"in house" survey	children in care	all ages mostly school age
Raynor 1970, UK (See also Gill & Jackson)	51	pros-spective (action research)	black children mostly placed trans-racially	under 2 yrs
Reich & Lewis 1986, UK	69; 47*	pros-pective	all special needs - mostly handi-capped	all ages

*69 referred; 47 placed

Author and Country	Size of sample	Type of study	Special Needs	Age at p'ment
Rowe et al. 1983, 1984 UK	145; 105*	retro-spective	children in care	all ages - mostly under 5 yrs.

*145 long-term foster care; 105 adopted by foster parents

Type of p'ment	Time in placement at time of study	Definition of success and success rates
adopted by foster parents or "strangers"	15 months	100% of those adopted by new families. 93% of those adopted by foster parents still in placement. Well-being same for both groups. Related to "sense of permanence".
adoption	6 months-4 years, and 6 years later	Majority of parents were satisfied. Few problems identified.
adoption by foster parents or "strangers"	1-4 years	97% still in placement. 73% of parents rate own satisfaction as excellent or good.
adoption and permanent fostering	12 months-5 years	5% of those under 10 at placement and 22% of those aged 10 or over experienced disruption
adoption	1-4 years	Ratings of adjustment based on detailed questionnaire and parents' views. 84% rated as having made a good adjustment.
adoption	2 years	87% of those placed still in placement at 2-year stage. 59% of those referred still in placement. Over 80% of placements rated as appropriate.
long-term foster care or adoption by foster parents	at least 3 years	Well-being of children. Satisfaction of foster parents. 70% of foster children gave no cause for concern compared with 89% of adopted children.

Author and Country	Size of sample	Type of study	Special Needs	Age at p'ment
Shireman & Johnson 1986, USA	118	longi-tudinal	black children placed with single black parents, or white parents	under 3 yrs.
Simon & Altstein 1977, 1981, USA	294 and 133	longi-tudinal/ pros-pective	black or of mixed parentage placed trans-racially	under 5 yrs.
Thoburn et al. 1986, 1989 UK *29 referred; 21 placed.	29; 21*	longi-tudinal	older or handicapped	6 mos.-15 yrs. average 9 yrs.
Thoburn & Rowe 1988, UK	1,165	retro-spective survey	general population of "special needs"	6 mos.-16 yrs.
Tizard, 1977; Hodges & Tizard, 1989, UK *(comparison groups of children restored to parents; and of middle-class children)	35	longi-tudinal/ pros-pective*	older children who spent between 2 and 7 years in institutions	2-7 yrs. (most under 5)
Triseliotis 1983, UK	40	retro-spective	older, poor parenting in early years	6 mos.-9 yrs.
Triseliotis & Russell, 1984 UK	44	retro-spective	older, poor parenting in early years	3-7 yrs. most under 5 yrs.

Type of p'ment	Time in placement at time of study	Definition of success and success rates
adoption	when aged 4 and 8	None had disrupted. Adjustment of 79% rated excellent or good. All had good sense of racial identity.
adoption	8-9 years for second study	Parents' reports on problems and sense of identity. 80% of adopters did not report significant problems.
adoption and permanent fostering	at 18 months to 2 years, and 5 years	Varied between 50% and 100% depending on definition of success used. 86% still in placement. 72% of those referred still in placement. 80% rated as very successful or fairly successful.
adoption or permanent fostering	18 months - 5 years	79% of children still in placement. Breakdown rate increases with age at placement.
30 adopted; 5 permanently fostered	aged 4, 8 and 16 years	100% of children still in placement at age of 8. A range of other criteria used to assess parental satisfaction and child's well-being. 80% of parents satisfied or very satisfied.
long-term fostering	average 11 years	"An insignificant number" broke down. 70% of young adults were satisfied or fairly satisfied.
adoption	most of their childhood	82% of young adults rated their experience of growing up positively. Over 80% had made a good adjustment.

Author and Country	Size of sample	Type of study	Special Needs	Age at p'ment
Wedge 1986, UK	94	retro-spective survey	mostly older or handicapped children in care	all ages
Wedge & Mantle 1988, UK	133	retro-spective survey	siblings placed together or separately	all ages average 7 yrs.
Wolkind & Kozaruk 1983, 1986 UK	108	retro-spective	medical and developmental problems	all ages average 3 yrs.

Type of p'ment	Time in placement at time of study	Definition of success and success rates
adoption or permanent fostering	6 months - 30 months	80% were still in placement.
adoption or permanent fostering	18 months - 5 years	79% still in placement.
adoption	3 years	95% still in placement. Lower well-being ratings for children over 5 at placement.

Bibliography

Aldgate, J., (1980) 'Identification of Factors which influence Length of Stay in Care' in J.P. Triseliotis, New Developments in Foster Care and Adoption, London, Routledge and Kegan Paul.

Argent, H., (ed.) (1988) Keeping the doors open, London, BAAF.

Barth, R., Berry, M., Carson, M., Goodfield, R. and Feinberg, B. (1986) 'Contributors to disruption and dissolution of older-child adoptions', Child Welfare, vol. 65, no. 4.

Barth, R. and Berry, M., (1987) 'Outcomes of child welfare services under permanency planning', Social Services Review, March.

Berridge, D. and Cleaver, H., (1987) Foster home breakdown, Oxford, Blackwell.

Bohman, M., (1970) Adopted children and their families. A follow-up study of adopted children, their background, environment and adjustment, Stockholm, Proprins.

Bohman, M. and Sigvardsson, S., (1978) 'Long-term effects of early institutional care: a prospective longitudinal study' in Journal of Child Psychology and Psychiatry, vol. 20.

Bohman, M. and Sigvardsson, S., (1980) 'Negative social heritage', Adoption and Fostering, vol. 101, no. 3.

Bowlby, J., (1979) The making and breaking of affectional bonds, London, Tavistock.

Cairns, B., (1984) 'The children's family trust: a unique approach to substitute family care?, British Journal of Social Work, vol. 14.

Clarke, A., (1981) 'Adoption Studies', Adoption and Fostering, vol. 104, no. 2.

Clarke, A.M. and Clarke, A.D.B., (1976) Early experience: myth and evidence, London, Open Books.

Corcoran, A., (1988) 'Open adoption: the child's right', Adoption and Fostering, vol. 12, no. 3.

Coyne, A. and Brown, M., (1985) 'Developmentally disabled children can be adopted,, Child Welfare, vol.64, no. 6.

Department of Health and Social Security, (1983) Code of Practice on Access to Children in Care, London, HMSO.

Department of Health and Social Security, (1985a) Social work decisions in child care: Recent research findings and their implications, London, HMSO.

Department of Health and Social Security, (1985b) Review of child care law, London, HMSO.

Department of Health and Social Security, (1987) The law on child care and family services, Cm.62, London, HMSO.

Donley, K., (1975) Opening New Doors, London, ABAA.

Fanshel, D., (1972) Far from the reservation: the transracial adoption of American Indian children, Metuchen, N.J., Scarecrow.

Fanshel, D. and Shinn, E.B. (1978) Children in Foster Care - A Longitudinal Study, New York, Columbia University Press.

Fein, E., Davies, L. and Knight, G., (1979) 'Placement stability in foster care', Social Work, vol. 24.

Fein, E., Maluccio, A.N., Hamilton, V.J., and Ward, D.E., (1983) 'After Foster Care: Permanency Planning for Children', Child Welfare, vol. 62, no. 6.

Festinger, T., (1983) No one ever asked us ... A postscript to foster care, New York, Columbia University Press.

Festinger, T., (1986) Necessary risk: A study of adoptions and disrupted adoptive placements, New York, Child Welfare League of America.

Fisher, M., Marsh, P. and Phillips, D. with Sainsbury, E., (1986) In and out of care: the experiences of children, parents and social workers, London, Batsford/BAAF.

Fitzgerald, J., (1983) Understanding Disruption, London, BAAF.

Fitzgerald, J., Murcer, B. and Murcer, B., (1982) Building New Families through Adoption and Fostering, Oxford, Blackwell.

Fratter, J., Newton, D. and Shinegold, D., (1982) Cambridge Cottage Pre-Fostering and Adoption Unit, Barkingside, Essex, Barnardo Social Work Papers, no.16.

George, V., (1970) Foster Care, London, Routledge and Kegan Paul.

Gill, O. and Jackson, B., (1983) Adoption and race, London, Batsford/BAAF.

Grow, L.J. and Shapiro, D., (1974) Black children-white parents. A study of transracial adoption, New York, Child Welfare League of America.

Grow, L.J. and Shapiro, D., (1975) Transracial adoption today. New York, Child Welfare League of America.

Haimes, E. and Timms, N., (1985) Adoption, Identity, and Social Policy, Aldershot, Gower.

Hapgood, M., (1984) 'Older child adoption and the knowledge base of adoption practice' in Bean, P. (ed.) Adoption: Essays in social policy law, and sociology, London, Tavistock.

Hart, G.J., (1986) Entitled to our care: A study of an adoption agency placing children with special needs, Salford, University of Salford, Department of Sociology and Anthropology.

Hazel, N., (1981) A Bridge to Independence, Oxford, Blackwell.

Herbert, M., (1984) 'Causes and treatment of behaviour problems in adoptive children' in Bean, P. (ed.) Adoption: Essays in social policy law, and sociology, London, Tavistock.

Hill, M. and Triseliotis, J., (1986) Adoption allowances in Scotland: The first five years, Edinburgh, Social Work Services Group.

HMSO, (1968) Report of the Committee of Inquiry appointed to review the Organisation and Responsibilities of the Local Authority Personal Social Services in England and Wales, (Seebohm Report), HMSO, London.

Hodges, J. and Tizard, B., (1989) 'Social and family relationships of ex-institutional adolescents', Journal of Child Psychology and Psychiatry, vol. 30, no.1.

Hodges, J. and Tizard, B., (1989a) 'IQ and behavioural adjustment of ex-institutional adolescents', Journal of Child Psychology and Psychiatry, vol.30, no. 1.

Hoksbergen, R.A.C., Juffer, F. and Waardenburg , B.C., (1987) Adopted children at home and school, Utrecht, Swets and Zeitlinger.

Hoksbergen, R.A.C., Waardenburg, B.C. and Spaan, J.T.T.M., (1987) Under standing and preventing disruption. Paper presented to the International Conference on Adoption, Athens.

Holman, R., (1975) 'The place of fostering in social work", British Journal of Social Work, vol.5, no.1.

Hornby, H.C., (1986) 'Why adoptions disrupt', Children Today, New York.

Howe, D., (1987a) 'Adoption trends and counter-trends, in Adoption and Fostering, vol. 11, no. 1.

Howe, D., (1987b) 'Adopted children in care', British Journal of Social Work, vol. 17.

Howe, D., (1988) 'Survey of initial referrals to the Post-Adoption Centre', Adoption and Fostering, vol. 12, no. 1.

Howe, D. and Hinings, D., (1987) 'Adopted children referred to a child and family centre', Adoption and Fostering, vol. 11, no. 3.

Humphrey, M., (1963) 'Factors associated with maladjustment in adoptive families, Child Adoption, vol. 43.

Hussell, C. and Monaghan, B., (1982) 'Child Care Planning in Lambeth, Adoption and Fostering, vol. 6, no. 2.

Jacka, A., (1973) Adoption in brief, Windsor, NFER.

Jaffee, B. and Fanshel, D., (1970) How they fared in adoption: a follow-up study, New York, Columbia University Press.

Jenkins, R., (1969) 'Long-term fostering', Case Conference, vol.15, no.9.

Jewett, C.L., (1978) Adopting the Older Child, Harvard, The Harvard Common Press.

Jewett, C.L., (1984) Helping children cope with separation and loss, London, Batsford/BAAF.

Jones, M.A., (1985) A second chance for families: Five years later - Follow-up of a program to prevent foster care, New York, Child Welfare League of America.

Kadushin, A., (1970) Adopting Older Children, New York, Columbia University Press.

Kadushin, A. and Seidl, F.W., (1971) 'Adoption failure: A social work postmortem', Social Work, July.

Kagan, R. and Reid, W., (1986) 'Critical factors in the adoption of emotionally disturbed youths', Child Welfare, vol. 65, 1.

Katz, L., (1986) 'Parental stress and factors for success in older child adoption', Child Welfare, vol. 65, no. 6.

Kaye, E. and Tipton, M., (1985) Evaluation of State activities with regard to adoption disruption, Washington, Office of Human Development Services.

Kerrane, A., Hunter, A. and Lane, M., (1980) Adopting older and handicapped children, London, Barnardo's.

Kirk, D., (1964) Shared fate, London, Collier-Macmillan.

Kornitzer, M., (1968) Adoption and family life, London, Putnam.

Krementz, J., (1982) How it feels to be adopted, London, Victor Gollancz.

Lahti J., (1982) 'A follow-up study of foster children in permanent placements', Social Service Review, University of Chicago.

Lambert, L. and Streather, J., (1980) Children in Changing Families, London, Macmillan.

Lindsay-Smith, C. and Price, E., (1980) Barnardo's New Families Project - Glasgow: The First Two Years, Barkingside, Essex, Barnardo's Social Work Papers, no. 13.

Lynch, M. and Roberts, J., (1982) Consequences of Child Abuse, London, Academic Press.

Macaskill, C., (1985a) Against the odds. Adopting mentally handicapped children, London, BAAF.

Macaskill, C., (1985b) 'Post-adoption support' and 'Who should support after adoption?' in Adoption and Fostering, vol. 9, no. 1 and vol. 9, no. 2.

McKay, M., (1980) 'Planning for permanent placement', Adoption and Fostering, vol.4, no. 1.

McWhinnie, A., (1967) Adopted Children: How they grow up, London, Routledge and Kegan Paul.

Maluccio, A.N., Fein, E., Hamilton, J., Klier, J.L. and Ward, D., (1980) 'Beyond permanency planning', Child Welfare, vol.59.

Maluccio, A.N. and Fein, E. (1983) 'Permanency planning revisited' in Cox, M. and Cox, R. (eds.) Foster care: current issues and practices, New Jersey, Ablex Press.

Maluccio, A.N. and Fein, E., (1983) 'Permanency planning: A redefinition', Child Welfare, vol. 62, no. 3.

Maluccio, A.N. and Fein, E., (1985) 'Growing up in foster care', Children and Youth Services Review, vol. 7.

Maluccio, A.N., Fein, E. and Olmstead, K.A., (1986) Permanency planning for children: concepts and methods, London, Tavistock.

Mann, P., (1984) Children in Care Revisited, London, Batsford.

Maza, P., (1985) 'What we do - and don't - know about adoption statistics', Permanency Report, Spring.

Millham, S., Bullock, R., Hosie, K. and Haak, M., (1986) Lost in care. Aldershot, Gower.

Morris, C., (1984) The Permanency Principle in Child Care Social Work, Norwich, Social Work Monographs, University of East Anglia.

Napier, M., (1972) 'Success and failure in foster care', British Journal of Social Work, vol. 2, no. 2.

National Children's Bureau, (1985) Parents for children: Some findings from a research project, London, National Children's Bureau.

Nelson, K.A., (1985) On the frontier of adoption: A study of special-needs adoptive families, Washington, Child Welfare League of America.

O'Hara, J. and Hoggan, P., 'Permanent substitute family care in Lothian - placement outcomes', Adoption and Fostering, vol. 12, no. 3.

Packman, J., (1981) The Child's Generation (Second Edition). Oxford, Blackwell.

Packman, J. with Randall, J. and Jacques, N., (1986) Who needs care? Social work decisions about children, Oxford, Basil Blackwell.

Parents for Children, (1981, 1982, 1983) Annual Reports, London, Parents for Children.

Parker, R.A., (1966) Decision in Child Care, London, Allen and Unwin.

Parker, R.A., (1980) Caring for Separated Children, London, Macmillan.

Parkinson, L., (1986) Conciliation in separation and divorce, London, Croom Helm.

Powell, J.Y., (1984) Adults who were adopted as older children, Ann Arbor, University Microfilms International.

Pringle, M.L.K., (1967) Adoption - Facts and Fallacies, London, Longman.

Proch, K., (1982) 'Differences between foster care and adoption: Perceptions of adopted foster children and adoptive foster parents', Child Welfare, vol. 6, no. 5.

Raynor, L., (1970) Adoption of non-white children, London, Allen and Unwin.

Raynor, L., (1980) The adopted child comes of age, London, Allen and Unwin.

Reid, W., Kagan, R., Kaminsky, A. and Helmer, K., (1987) 'Adoptions of older institutionalised youth', Social Casework.

Rowe, J., (1983) Fostering in the eighties, London, BAAF.

Rowe, J. and Lambert, L., (1973) Children Who Wait, London, ABAA.

Rowe, J., Hundleby, M., Paul, H. and Keane, A., (1980 and 1981) 'Long-term Fostering and the Children Act 1975', Adoption and Fostering, vol. 102, no. 4; vol. 103, no. 1.

Rowe, J., Cain, H., Hundleby, M., Keane, A., (1984) Long-Term Foster Care, London, Batsford.

Rowe, J., Hundleby, M. and Garnett, L., (1988) Child Care Now - A survey of placement patterns, Report to DHSS, London.

Rushton, A. and Treseder, J., (1986) 'Developmental recovery', Adoption and Fostering, vol.10, no.3.

Rushton, A., Treseder, J. and Quinton, D. (1988), New Parents for Older Children, London, BAAF.

Rutter, M.(1975) 'Attainment and adjustment in two geographical areas', British Journal of Psychiatry, no. 126.

Sachdev, P. (ed.) (1987) Adoption: Current issues and trends, Vancouver, Butterworths.

Sainsbury, E., Nixon, S. and Phillips, D., (1982) Social work in Focus: Clients' and Social Workers' Perceptions in Long-Term Social Work, London, Routledge and Kegan Paul.

Sawbridge, P., (1980) 'Seeking new parents: A decade of development, Triseliotis,J.P. (ed.), New Developments in Foster Care and Adoption, London: Routledge and Kegan Paul.

Sawbridge, P., (1983) Parents for Children. Twelve practice papers, London, BAAF.

Sawbridge, P., (1988) 'The Post-Adoption Centre', Adoption and Fostering, vol.12, no.3.

Seglow, J., Pringle, M.L.K. and Wedge, P., (1972) Growing up adopted. London, NFER.

Seltzer, M. and Bloksberg, L., (1987) 'Permanency planning and its effects on foster children: A review of the literature', Social Work, Jan. 12.

Shaw, M., (1984) 'Growing up adopted' in Bean, P. (ed.) Adoption: Essays in social policy, law and sociology, London, Tavistock.

Shaw, M., (1987) Family placement for children in care: A guide to the literature, London, BAAF.

Shaw, M. and Hipgrave, T., (1983) Specialist Fostering, London, Batsford.

Shireman, J. and Johnson, P., (1986) 'A longitudinal study of black adoptions', Social Work, May-June.

Simon, R.J. and Altstein, H., (1977) Transracial adoption, New York, Wiley.

Simon, R.J. and Altstein, H., (1981) Transracial adoption: A follow-up, Lexington, Lexington Books.

Stein, M. and Carey, K., (1986) Leaving Care, Oxford, Basil Blackwell.

Stein, T.J., Gambrill, E.D. and Wiltse, K.T., (1978) Children in foster homes: achieving continuity of care, New York, Praeger.

Stroud, J,, (1960) The Shorn Lamb, London, Longmans.

Thoburn, J., (1980) Captive Clients, London, Routledge and Kegan Paul.

Thoburn, J., (1985) 'What kind of permanence', Adoption and Fostering, vol. 9, no. 4.

Thoburn, J., (1988) Child Placement: Principles and Practice, Aldershot, Gower/Wildwood.

Thoburn, J., Murdoch, A. and O'Brien, A., (1986) Permanence in child care, Oxford, Basil Blackwell.

Thoburn, J. and Rowe, J., (1988) 'A snapshot of permanent family placement', Adoption and Fostering, vol.12, no.3.

Thorpe, R., (1980) 'The experience of parents and children living apart' in Triseliotis, J.P. (ed.) New developments in foster care and adoption, London, Routledge and Kegan Paul.

Tizard, B., (1977) Adoption, a Second Chance, London, Open Books.

Trasler, G., (1960) In place of parents, London, Routledge and Kegan Paul.

Triseliotis, J.P., (1973) In search of origins, London, Routledge and Kegan Paul.

Triseliotis, J.P., (1983) 'Identity and security in adoption and long-term fostering', Adoption and Fostering, vol.7, no. 1.

Triseliotis, J.P., (1986) 'Older children in care' in Wedge, P. and Thoburn, J. Finding families for "hard-to-place" children, London, BAAF.

Triseliotis, J.P. and Russell, J., (1984) Hard to Place - The outcome of adoption and residential care, Aldershot, Gower.

Vernon, J. and Fruin, D., (1986) In care: A study of social work decision making, London, National Children's Bureau.

Wedge, P., (1986) 'Family finding in Essex' in Wedge, P. and Thoburn, J. (eds.), Finding families for "hard-to-place" children: evidence from research, London, BAAF.

Wedge, P. and Thoburn, J. (eds.) (1986) Finding families for "hard-to-place" children: evidence from research, London, BAAF.

Wedge, P. and Mantle, G. (in preparation) The placement of sibling groups with permanent substitute families, Norwich, University of East Anglia.

Weinstein, E., (1960) The self-image of the foster child New York, Sage.

Wolkind, S. and Kozaruk, A., (1983) 'The Adoption of Children with Medical Handicap', Adoption and Fostering, vol.7, no. 1.

Wolkind, S. and Kozaruk, A., (1986) '"Hard-to-place?" Children with medical and developmental problems' in Wedge, P. and Thoburn, J. (eds.) Finding families for "hard-to-place" children, London, BAAF.

Index